MY $TREET

MONEY

**A Street-Level View
of Managing Your Money
From the Heart to the Bank**

Louis Barajas

Financial Greatness, Inc.
Los Angeles, CA

Library of Congress Control Number: 2010942531

Cataloging information
ISBN-10 098304600X
ISBN-13 978-0983046004

Printed in the United States of America

Contents

This book is dedicated to
four great women who are
helping me inspire the people on My Street:
Sarah Barajas, Angie Barajas,
Mary DiMaggio and Victoria St. George

From the Heart to the Bank,
All Finance is Personal

When it comes to finances and financial expertise, most people don't think of the heart first. But then again, I'm not your typical financial expert. First of all, I grew up in East Los Angeles, a community where families struggle to make ends meet yet they are rich in the things that matter. My father emigrated from Mexico and worked two jobs to support his wife and his family. In 1972 I was 11 years old, and my brother had just been born. The United States was going through a recession, and one night my dad walked in, sat down at the kitchen table and told us he had lost one of his jobs. A friend of his had given him a welding machine and to take care of our family, out of necessity he was going to start a wrought iron business. Because his English wasn't good, he asked if I could help him with his paperwork. So at age 11 I filled out his business application, did his books, and helped my dad in any way I could.

A couple of years later, my dad was getting customers in some of the more affluent communities in Los Angeles. One day he took me on a job he had in Beverly Hills. It was a big house with a beautiful car parked in the driveway.

"Dad, how do people get to live like this?" I asked.

"It's got to be education," he answered. At that moment I resolved that I would graduate from college and do well for myself and my family. When I graduated from high school, I received a scholarship to UCLA. I was the first person in my family to go to college—and it wasn't easy. UCLA was a completely different world from East Los Angeles. No one on my street knew the first thing about going to a university, living in a dorm, studying tough subjects, managing your time, and getting to know people from very different backgrounds. I felt very lonely, but I was determined to succeed. I graduated from UCLA with a degree in sociology and then went to Claremont Graduate University School of Management to get my MBA. But in the back of my mind I kept the goal of helping my dad with his business—only now my vision had expanded, to include helping people like my dad to take care of themselves financially.

A friend suggested that I become a financial planner, and that seemed like the perfect career choice. I went to work with a large company whose mission was "to offer financial planning for the middle class." Perfect! I thought—only to quickly discover that their true mission was to *sell* financial products to the middle class, whether their customers needed the products or not. And that didn't work for me. I became the number one financial planner in my office and sold the most plans, but the fewest products. My customers needed checking and savings accounts, not annuities! But the company put constant pressure on me to sell more. So I resigned, and I joined a prestigious accounting firm in Newport Beach, California. While working there I studied to become a Certified Public Accountant. Only a couple of years out of graduate school, and I had a good job with a healthy income. I had a nice house in Orange County; I got married; I was like those people whose home in Beverly Hills I had so admired. Life was good—wasn't it?

My wake-up call came in 1990, when my grandmother passed away. She had been the love of my life and we were incredibly close, and her death was very difficult for me. Then, just a short time later, my uncle, her eldest son, Frank Medina, who had taught me to love books and encouraged my passion for learning, committed suicide. Losing these two people was a watershed moment in my life. I questioned everything. I didn't know what was important anymore. That same year my first daughter was born. The morning after her birth I had a chance conversation with a pastor in a coffee shop in Lake Forest, California. We talked about living a life of purpose. That conversation helped me clarify what was really important to me. I remembered that I had always wanted to serve people whom I felt really needed good, solid financial advice. They were the teachers, the city employees, and the owners of small businesses in underserved areas. They had been my neighbors while I was growing up, and we still shared the same concerns and needs. I wanted to show them how to create financial success in the communities in which they were living, keeping in mind all of the things that were most important—family, friends, giving back.

Shortly after my daughter's birth I walked into my Newport Beach office and resigned. I had found my purpose in life and was determined to carry it out. I knew it would be difficult to start from scratch, but I decided I would open a financial planning business in East Los Angeles. I created a plan to get my business started—it would require sacrifice, but it would allow me to live my purpose. I slept in one of the apartments over my dad's business and spent weeks going through the neighborhood, handing out fliers to everyone I met, advertising my services. I quickly discovered that even though the idea of financial planning was completely foreign to most of my neighbors, many of them needed someone to prepare their taxes. So that's what I did. I would do people's personal and business tax returns and then tell them, "If you want, we can create a financial plan that will reduce your taxes and help you keep more of your hard-earned money." A few of them took me up on the offer, then a few more. Eventually I was able to build a team: I hired an assistant, and then another financial planner. I checked my progress and decided I needed new ways to attract more people to my business. So I started offering Saturday seminars at the local library to talk to people about taxes and managing their money. I was building my own small business just like my father had, one client at a time. I had great confidence in my purpose and in my ability to make my dream come true, and I was truly grateful for all that I was building.

However, as I worked with people it became very clear that any financial advice I gave them also needed to fit into the bigger picture of their lives. I discovered that most of us have all kinds of beliefs and hang-ups about money that keep us from being confident about our finances, and we need to address these barriers before we try to earn, budget, or invest what we have. Ultimately, I wanted people to understand that what my parents had taught me was true—money is simply a means to an end, the "end" being all the different parts of our lives that we consider the most meaningful. Things like Family. Friends. Community. Faith. Health. Satisfying work. Being able to give your family a comfortable and happy home, free from financial worry and stress. The focus of my business changed from simply setting up financial plans for people to advising them on how they could use finances to help them achieve what they wanted most in life. I wanted to create meaningful conversations about money that would work for real people in real situations. My goal was to offer financial guidance from the street-level—not Wall Street, but My Street, the street on which most of us live, play, love, and work.

That's what I've been doing for over two decades. During that time I've written several books, including *The Latino Journey to Financial Greatness, Small Business, Big Life, and Overworked, Overwhelmed, and Underpaid*. I've become a recognized financial and small business expert, regularly interviewed by newspapers and magazines, and appearing on local and national TV and radio programs. Just like my clients, however, I've gone through highs and lows. I've faced the challenges of being an entrepreneur. I've been divorced and remarried; today my wife, Angie, and I have a blended family of three wonderful kids. I've seen boom times and recessions and helped people to do their best in both. I've advised successful athletes, celebrities, businesspeople, entrepreneurs, and pillars of society. I've held the hands of families who have lost loved ones and then came to me to help them figure out what to do next. I myself have lost a grandmother, an uncle, and a father-in-law. None of them were rich financially, but they touched the hearts of many people, and in that way they were rich beyond measure. After all these experiences, I've discovered that most of us don't particularly need to be rich. All we really want and need is to feel we have enough to take care of ourselves and our families, to provide a safe, secure, happy life for them now and in the future. We want money to fulfill our heart's desires, not the money itself. And we want a little bit of confidence that we can take care of ourselves and our families in both good and bad times.

I also discovered that it's easy to talk about finances when things are going well, when the stock market is going up, your retirement accounts are healthy, your house is rising in value, when you have a good, steady job and you're bringing home enough to take care of your family and put some money aside for the future. It's easy to talk about finances when you're living in a nice community where most people make over $100,000. But it's a lot harder to talk intelligently about finances when things are tough, when people are struggling just to get by, when financial security seems like a goal that is out of reach for the average person. That's when you need to remember why to have money. That's when you need to focus on what's truly important to you, and how money is only a means to get it. Instead of starting with money, we need to start from the heart—because that's what truly makes the biggest difference.

This is not your typical financial planning book. My purpose is to change the mindset of America—all of us who don't live on Wall Street or even Main Street, but who are going through tough times on the streets where we live. Yes, I have advice to give you about managing your money and setting up your life so you can be happy, live comfortably, retire securely, and leave something for your kids. But I don't plan to give you a bunch of investment recommendations. First of all, I can't—as a Certified Financial Planner™, it would be irresponsible of me to give you specific advice unless I knew your specific financial situation. But I believe that what you will learn from this book is far more important. It is designed, first, to help you get clear on what your heart wants, and second, to show you how to maximize your money to get your heart's desires. Because ultimately, the value of your time here on earth will have nothing to do with how much money you make and everything to do with how you choose to live, who you choose to love, and how you choose to make a difference.

Imagine that we all could stop fixating on the size of our bank balance, house value, or retirement account, and start using our resources to live better lives today while we prepare for tomorrow. Imagine that we could go from living a stressful life (focused only on what we don't have) to a successful life (where we celebrate our blessings and continually take small, consistent steps to build a better future). I believe you wouldn't be reading this book if you weren't ready to discover how you can live an abundant life rich in both money and heart. I will be honored if you let me be your guide.

1

A View From My Street, Not Wall Street

In the fall of 2008 I was being interviewed on CNN. If you remember, at that time it seemed the entire U.S. economy was melting down. Banks and big companies were going under, and no one had much of an idea of how we were going to make it through. The anchorperson said to me, "We're hearing all about what's happening on Wall Street—but as a financial expert for regular people, you deal with the real world. Tell us about Main Street. What's happening there?"

That was the first time I said it. "People that I talk to, they don't want to know about Wall Street or even Main Street—they want to know what's happening on *My* Street, on the street where they live," I told him. "And on My Street, people are worried. They're worried about their kids, they're worried about the cost of health care, they're worried about Social Security being there for them and their kids when it's time for them to retire. The people on My Street are the heart of this country, and it's time someone started looking out for them."

I've spent over two decades as a financial adviser to the people who live on "My Street" all across the United States. In that time I've discovered that My Street isn't a residential district or a commercial area or even an enterprise zone—it's a *neighborhood*, the place where people just like you and me live, work, play, have barbecues, share stories, laugh and cry. My Street is where we grow up, go to school, date, marry, and raise our kids; it's where together we mourn our losses and celebrate the happy moments of each other's lives.

You're one of the people on My Street if you....

  » Work long and hard to take care of your family and put a little aside so you can help your children go to college and live with some kind of security and dignity when you get old.

  » Make tough choices; you sacrifice many small and large pleasures today so you and your children will have a better tomorrow.

  » Have no desire to own a mansion; you just want to have a little extra money so you can travel with your family, or redo your kitchen, or maybe add an extra bedroom for a new baby or an aging parent.

  » Want peace of mind and the feeling that your hard work will be rewarded.

  » Understand that there's a lot more wealth to be found in your relationships and in the ways we pull together as a community than in the value of your home or the size of your retirement account.

  » Care about creating stability, success, and happiness for yourself and your loved ones.

On My Street today, many families are just one paycheck or illness or accident away from real financial problems. But on My Street, people still dream—and while their dreams are rooted in reality, they're just as important as any mega-millionaire's fantasies of building a financial empire. In fact, the dreams of the people on My Street are *more* important, because they have been powering the economic engine of the United States for centuries. I believe that people who work hard deserve respect and a measure of financial security and dignity. I also believe that the people on My Street deserve the kind of expert advice and information that will help them build a life of financial stability, security, and success.

Let me give you an example of what I mean. Not too long ago "Linda" asked me to help her make some headway with her finances. Linda was in her thirties, divorced, with two children under the age of ten. She had been renting a condo since she and her husband had split up, but the condo's owner wanted to sell the property. Linda didn't know what to do. Should she try to rent another condo in the same area so her kids wouldn't have to change schools? Should she put in a bid to buy the condo she was living in? Did she have enough money to afford a down payment *and* to finance a mortgage? Linda worked for the state of California, and she had a good job—only for the past year all state workers had had to take every other Friday off, without pay, due to budget cuts. In effect, Linda's pay had been cut by 15 percent, and there was no guarantee she would receive a pay raise anytime in the future. Linda had her state pension, but because of the expenses of the divorce she had very little other savings. She wanted to put money aside for her kids' education, but she hadn't figured out a way to squeeze anything extra out of her already stretched budget.

The stress of her situation was keeping Linda up at night. Like a lot of people in tight financial straits, she felt she had nowhere to turn. "I feel like we're living on the edge," she told me. "My daughter went to the dentist last month and he's recommending she get braces. How can I afford that? And my son, Jimmy, sprained his ankle playing football. The visit to the emergency room was only partially covered by our health insurance, so now I have a bill for $500 sitting on my desk. And then I get the note from my landlord that we either have to buy the condo or move. It's just too much!" Linda was close to tears because she saw no way out of her situation. "I do my best to take care of my family. Why does it have to be so hard?" she asked.

Many of us on My Street are doing our best to do the right thing. We go to work, pay our bills on time, watch our expenses, save for the future, only to be confronted with personal, professional, and financial emergencies that seem to threaten everything we have. But there can be light at the end of the tunnel, if we take a few moments, first, to get perspective—see clearly where we are and what's really important; second, to create a workable plan that takes into account our needs as well as our wants; and third, to follow that plan consistently until we reach our goals.

I started by reassuring Linda, "You've done the best you could with what you have. Now you need to make it a priority to stay calm and focused. How long do you have before you either need to move or put in an offer on your condo?"

Linda took a deep breath. "The landlord said he was going to put the condo on the market next month but that I could put in an offer before he lists it."

"So our first priority is to help you decide if you want to stay, if you can afford to buy at this point in time, and if this condo is at the right price for you," I reminded her. "We can do that by taking you through a very simple series of questions and looking carefully at your income, your financial situation, and what you want in a home. By the way, there are programs designed to help first-time homebuyers, so you may be able to get financial assistance with both your down payment and mortgage."

Linda's face brightened. "Really? And you can help me figure out the best decision to make about the condo?"

"Absolutely," I said. "And it will be the best decision based on your overall life goals, not just your short-term needs. After all, would you want to buy the condo if it meant you'd have to get a second job to afford the payments, or pull your kids out of band or camp or football because there's no money?"

Linda shook her head. "I'd rather move to a smaller place than make them give up everything they enjoy."

"Linda, most of us don't do a lot of planning, either for our finances or our lives," I told her. "We just fall into habits that may or may not help us create the lives we want. But with a little attention, effort, planning, and understanding of what's really important, we each can make better use of what we have to take care of our families and ourselves. Let's figure out a plan that will help you create a great life for you and your kids." Based on our discussions, Linda decided to move into a smaller unit in the same complex and to put the money she saved on rent each month toward saving for a down payment. Within a year, she was able to use her savings and a local first-time home buyer's assistance program to purchase a condo a few blocks away.

Helping Linda, and people just like her on My Street, inspires me and has motivated me for over two decades. I want to tackle the everyday money issues that people experience in their neighborhoods and in their small businesses. My goal is to help individuals handle their financial challenges and make good choices that will lead to better and more prosperous lives. I want to show people on My Street how to create new opportunities for themselves and their loved ones. That is the goal of this book.

My Street Money is about...

» Finding real-time money answers for real people.

» Learning what money can do to help you create a more meaningful life.

» Showing you how to experience less financial stress and worry, and live with more happiness instead.

» Creating the dignified life you desire and deserve.

» Helping your children get a head start in life to help them be more successful.

» Building strong, happy families that can weather tough times and celebrate the good times together.

Mindset, Money, and Meaning

If you ask most people on My Street what would give them greater financial success, stability, and happiness, they usually say, "More money." However, achieving security and success on My Street has less to do with external resources like money than it does with internal resources that we all possess. I saw this in my community: most people there came from poor families and never had the opportunity to be in environments where they could learn about creating wealth. But those who did well financially worked as hard on building their internal resources as they did on putting money away. I studied these people to learn what made them successful, and I found that they had mastered what I call the three M's—*mindset, money, and meaning.*

Mindset—When I speak with people, I often ask the question, "What's the difference between being poor and being broke?" People who see themselves as poor usually believe their condition is permanent; they see themselves as constantly struggling and not able to change their circumstances. However, "broke" is temporary. Donald Trump has been broke many times in his career, but he always believed he could make the money back and become rich again. This example demonstrates the power of *mindset* to shape our success. Through the years I have found that I could try to teach people about finances, but unless they had the right mindset they wouldn't be able to absorb the information. They had to believe that while finances might not be the easiest material to master, they were as capable as the next person of succeeding.

When you have the right mindset, it's easy to learn the lessons that will help you handle your finances successfully. On the other hand, if you have gone through financial challenges in the past, it can be difficult to "get your mind right" again so you can take advantage of opportunities and safeguard your hard-earned money. Much of this book is designed to help you develop the right mindset.

Money—This has far less to do with the amount of money you have and far more to do with your knowledge of how to *use* the money you possess. You need to know the basics of how finances work. There are essentially five things you must learn to do with your money: earn it, save it, spend it wisely, protect it, and invest it. Throughout this book you'll find information, examples, and suggestions that will help you develop knowledge and confidence in these five categories.

Meaning—The meaning you create around finances will determine what you are willing to do and how long you will persevere in doing it. Meaning includes all of your personal reasons for learning to master your finances—what money will give you, what it will mean for your family, your future, and your community. Meaning provides you with the inspiration and motivation to put in the work to earn, invest, and care for your money. When your mindset, knowledge of money, and meaning are positive and aligned with each other, you'll be able to use your resources in very powerful ways, and to overcome the inevitable challenges of life with strength and success. Most of this book is dedicated to helping you master the three "M's" so you can create an abundant, happy life for you and your family.

The Five Stages of "Making It" on My Street

To reach the financial security and success that we desire on My Street, most of us go through different stages. Some people may start at the very beginning, while others start closer to the goal. Here's what happens at each stage of the journey.

Survival—Many individuals find themselves in survival after losing a job, or going through other personal or professional challenges. At this stage people have trouble making plans beyond a day or a week because they don't think that they can change their present circumstances. However, the only way out of survival is to believe that a better future is possible, and to keep working every day to improve your situation.

Struggle—Here people have food on the table and a roof over their heads, but it wouldn't take much of a loss to put them back into survival again. Many people in this stage work hard because they are motivated by fear. At this point it's important to create a plan that will not only keep you out of survival but will help you keep building toward a better life.

Stability—At this stage people have a home, food on the table, they can pay their bills and begin to save for the future. For some people, stability can seem like the ultimate goal, especially if they've been stuck in survival or struggle for a long time. However, as many of us discovered, stability can be shaken all too easily by factors beyond our control. Stability should be the base of your financial foundation. It's where you start, not where you plan to finish.

Success—Here people own a home and a car or two; they have retirement savings and money set aside for their children's education; they can afford all the little extras that make life pleasant. Unfortunately, at this point many people can start to take their success for granted and make unwise decisions about their lives and their finances. Or they wake up and realize that the most important things in life aren't possessions. They realize that something is missing; and when they find it, they reach the true goal of the journey...

Financial Confidence— This is a mindset based on a clear vision of who you want to become and what you want to give, not just on how much money you have. Financial confidence occurs when people understand that money isn't the final measure of success, but a life of purpose is. It is having the courage to live the life of your dreams, knowing that your life matters, and having the faith to be grateful and share with others every step along the way.

If we're lucky, most of us rarely go through survival, where we don't even have a roof over our heads. Many of us do go through struggle when we're first starting out, and then hopefully we keep moving through stability, success, and ultimately financial confidence. But while each stage may have something important to teach us, we can bypass some of the steps of the journey to financial confidence simply by knowing *what* to do and *when* to do it. I believe we can learn lessons from the struggles of others, and use what we learn to shorten our journey. But we have to be willing to listen, learn, and then put what we learn into practice.

What's Really Important on My Street?

Unfortunately, many of us never take the time to figure out what's truly important to us. Today, right now, I invite you to stop and ask yourself a question: When you reach the end of your life, what will you be proudest of: the hours you put in at work, or the time you spent with the people you love? Will you look back and see wasted opportunities and feel regret, or will you celebrate the moments you shared and cared for others? Are you willing to put in a little time to plan your life now so you can create the life and future you truly want?

When it comes to happiness on My Street, I believe that the most important question is not, "How much money do you have saved?" but "Are you living a life of purpose, one where abundance flows naturally? Do you know who you are, what you have money for, and why?" Success and happiness on My Street doesn't come from money but from knowing why you want to earn it—your reasons for doing well in *all* areas of your life.

Getting a handle on your finances starts not with *how* you will handle money, but with *why*. Ask yourself: why do you want to save, invest, or set a spending plan? What non-monetary benefits will you receive if you learn to manage your money well? To get you thinking, here are a few ideas of ways you can benefit from taking charge of your finances:

» More confidence about your future.

» Able to take advantage of investment or career opportunities.

» Reduced stress. Able to sleep better.

» Better chances of a harmonious marriage. (The number one cause of divorce is financial stress.)

» Able to leave a bad situation/job/relationship.

» Able to take the time to find a good job if you are laid off or fired.

» Able to handle financial emergencies without having to resort to borrowing.

» Provide for your family's future, including education for your children.

» Able to retire when you want and still maintain your lifestyle.

I believe everyone on My Street deserves this kind of life. But to attain it, you must do three simple things. First, you must get out of your own way, by eliminating the beliefs and barriers that prevent you from recognizing your own strengths. Second, you need to understand the basics of making the most out of your financial resources. And third, you need a little confidence and courage, a willingness to step forward and claim your spot on the sunny side of My Street. My hope is that the ideas in this book will help you change your beliefs, maximize your money, and give you the confidence and courage to claim the life you deserve. These precepts can help you bring more money into your life and give you more peace of mind. And for those of us on My Street today, more money and a better night's sleep sound pretty darn good.

The Heart of the Matter

➤ Financial success requires that we get perspective—see clearly where we are and what's really important; create a workable plan that takes into account our needs as well as our wants; and follow that plan consistently until we reach our goals.

➤ To do well financially, you need to master the three M's: mindset, money, and meaning. You must develop the right mindset to learn about finances, you must know the basics of how finances work, and you must understand your personal reasons for mastering your finances now.

➤ There are five stages many people go through in their pursuit of financial success: survival, struggle, stability, success, and financial confidence. We can bypass some of these stages by learning from others and putting what we learn into practice.

➤ To create a great life on My Street, you must eliminate any beliefs that prevent you from recognizing your own strengths, understand the basics of making the most out of your financial resources, and be confident, courageous, and willing to do the work.

2

Wealth Begins in the Mind: Nine Beliefs that May Be Holding You Back

There's a story of an experiment conducted with a group of four monkeys placed in a room-sized cage. In the middle of the cage was a pole, from which hung a bunch of bananas. However, every time a monkey would try to climb the pole and get a banana, the monkey would be doused with cold water. Immediately the monkey would scamper away. Eventually all four monkeys gave up trying to reach for the bananas.

Here's the interesting part of the experiment: when the researchers replaced one of the monkeys and the new monkey would start to climb the pole to get a banana, the other three monkeys would pull it back down because they didn't want the new monkey to get hurt. After a few such attempts, the new monkey would give up. Eventually the researchers replaced every single monkey that had been doused with cold water—and still the remaining monkeys would pull down any animal who tried to get to the bananas, even though they themselves had never been penalized for trying to climb the pole. The hungry monkeys would look up at the bananas and want to climb the pole to reach the food, but they wouldn't. They didn't know why; they just thought that climbing the pole was bad. This is a clear example of the power of a *belief* to affect behavior. The monkeys believed that climbing the pole led to bad things, and therefore they wouldn't try to climb it to reach the bananas. Our lives, and our results, reflect our beliefs, because beliefs shape our perceptions.

Obviously, you and I aren't monkeys—but what if the "banana" affected by our beliefs concerned work, or money, or the ability to earn a good salary? What if someone believes that they can't make a six-figure income because they don't have an advanced degree, like a doctor or lawyer or C.P.A? What if someone believes they can't start a business because they don't have the time, money, advantages, or opportunities? What if a family tells a son or daughter not to take a job outside the country because it's too dangerous, or too far away? Or if another family doesn't want the main breadwinner to change professions because they're afraid it will mean a loss of income or status? Can you see how beliefs might keep people from pursuing their dreams?

Here's another example of the power of beliefs to shape perception and behavior. I frequently speak in high schools about money and finances, and it's pretty common to have a group of kids in the back of the auditorium who are talking, or texting, or roughhousing and disrupting the entire group. The best way to handle this is to say to the group, "I can walk into any classroom and tell you which students are going to be rich and which are going to be poor when they all grow up." Usually this gets the students' attention. Then I say, "A very wise man once said that poor people *know* everything while rich people *learn* everything. The students who are talking and not paying attention in class think they know everything already, but they're the ones who will end up poor. The rich ones will be those who are interested in learning whatever will help them succeed." It's amazing—after that comment, the kids in the back become quiet and start paying attention, because they believe that listening to me might just help them become wealthy.

Our beliefs—about ourselves, about money, about abundance—can either support us or get in our way when it comes to making the most of our financial resources. Beliefs can be positive or negative. Some examples of negative beliefs include "Money is the root of all evil," "To make a lot of money, you have to neglect your family," "Money doesn't grow on trees," "More money, more problems." "People who have a lot of money are called filthy rich for a reason." With a little digging, you'll probably find a version of at least one of these negative beliefs about money in your own mind. Yet at the same time most of us have other, more positive beliefs about money. Money helps us support our families. Money can make us more comfortable. Money can give us more choices. Money can pay for health care, travel, and retirement. Money can be used to benefit our children, charities, and our community. And you may have discovered, *not* having money can be very painful.

Many of our beliefs are learned from parents, friends, and our culture, and they are often based on wrong information and wrong assumptions. Incorrect beliefs can cause us to keep doing things the same way we've always done them, instead of exploring other ways to get better results. The greatest problems arise when those incorrect beliefs are about ourselves, our abilities, and what it will take for us to succeed financially. Take a look and see the results that your current beliefs have produced. Are you happy with what's going on in your financial life? Are there some places where you'd like more abundance but haven't been able to create it? Are there places where you know you have unresolved conflicts about money? If you're really committed to a life where your finances support you, your beliefs have to do the same.

But here's the good news: *You can choose to change your beliefs if they don't support you.* With a little knowledge and awareness of how you've been trained to think, and with a determination to break out of those old patterns, you can eliminate any old, negative beliefs that have been holding you back and adopt positive beliefs instead, beliefs that can help you build a solid financial future.

I have uncovered nine important beliefs that can damage your relationship to money. These beliefs are unconscious, but that gives them much greater power. As you read about each belief, ask yourself if it's one that you have, and then decide if you want to keep it.

Consider what this belief may cost you if you continue to hold on to it, and what new belief might help you create the financial future you desire. At the end of this chapter you'll learn a simple process for changing any limiting belief.

#1—Conflicting Beliefs About Money

Conflicting beliefs about anything prevent us from using the whole power of our minds and hearts to focus on what we want. If you want to make a lot of money but believe you'll have to sacrifice time with your family to earn it, how good will you feel about the extra income? Even when people have actually begun to succeed financially, their negative beliefs about money can make them unhappy. I've worked with individuals who worked very hard to reach a certain financial status, but then they start to get scared. They make stupid moves and sabotage their own efforts to increase their wealth. It's almost as if they have an internal "thermostat" that allows them to make only so much money before they have to "cool off."

Think about stories you may have heard about people who win the lottery: often they have trouble dealing with their sudden wealth and either lose it or fritter it away. They end up back at the same financial level they started. On the other hand, other people who lose all their money manage to make it back within a relatively short time. Why? I believe we all have a *financial comfort zone*, an amount of money or affluence we feel comfortable attaining. If we face setbacks that cause us to drop below a certain financial status, we'll work very hard to reach that level again. However, if things start getting too "hot"—if we make a lot of money, especially all of a sudden—then we may start doubting ourselves or feeling unworthy. We may overspend, or simply worry so much about money that we can't enjoy it. Eventually we sink back to the level of financial success where we feel comfortable.

No matter how much money we do or don't have, our beliefs about money will directly affect our relationship to it. However, what we believe about money is only true for us because we *believe* it, not because it's some universal truth. Money has no value in itself, but what we do with it creates the meaning it has in our lives. And what we believe about money will determine whether we master our money or money masters us.

In order to lower our stress around money and to ensure there are no obstacles to making it, managing it, and enjoying it, we must develop more positive beliefs around money. How? We need to remember all the *good* things that money can bring—greater freedom; greater peace of mind; increased security; more choices; the ability to contribute to our families, our communities, and ourselves at a higher level; the chance to take advantage of opportunities. We must respect money as a means to help us create a better quality of life, but we also must remember that money is a means to an end, not the end itself. After you meet your basic needs, more money doesn't necessarily make you happier. Money can't buy a beautiful sunset, or a hug from your child, or a laugh shared with your spouse, or tranquility at the end of a day well spent. All of these gifts are free, and they should be cherished more than anything money can buy.

#2—Depending on Others to Take Care of You

When we're children, we rightly expect that our parents will take care of our needs—putting food on the table, keeping a roof over our heads, buying our school supplies, and so on. Some of us may even be blessed with parents who can help put us through college. At some point, though, we have to take responsibility for ourselves and our future, both financial and otherwise. The problem is that some people believe that someone else will provide for their needs. I've heard people say, "My kids will take care of me when I retire," or "If I can't find a job after college, I can just live with my folks," or "So what if I don't have a lot of savings? There's plenty of time to save. Plus, I'll have Social Security to fall back on when I retire."

Most of us who have lived through the last few years are laughing through our tears right about now, because we've learned a very important lesson the hard way: *We can't rely on anyone else to take care of our finances.* We can't rely on our company continuing to have a job for us; we can't rely on a pension; Social Security may not be there when we retire. And because we're living longer, if we retire at age 65 (as most of us would like to), we can anticipate 25, even 35 years after that date when we will need to support ourselves without working. We *must* become self-reliant. We can't look to someone else to take care of our needs. There is no "they"—no government agency, welfare state, extended family, or divine providence—that we can count on. "God helps those that help themselves" is one important belief we all can adopt. And that means *we have to take financial responsibility for ourselves and our future, starting now.* We have to start saving for retirement as soon as possible, and put our money into investments we understand. We have to make our own plans and not rely on parents, children, employer, or the government to take care of us. I advise people to take advantage of their retirement plans at work, or set aside money every year in IRAs or other retirement savings vehicles. (Another way to build wealth for the future is to start your own business. If you are interested in starting a business, you should read my books on building a small business while creating a big life.) But no matter which path you choose to create wealth, you have to take responsibility for your own financial future.

#3—Effort vs. Reward: Working Harder Isn't Necessarily the Answer

Let's say you're working 40 hours a week and you make $50,000 a year—but to buy a house in your area and to put your children through college, you figure that you need to make $100,000 a year. Most people would think, "If I make $50,000 a year working 40 hours a week, to double my income I'd need to work twice as many hours. But I can't work 80 hours a week and have any kind of life!" But the "time = money" equation isn't always accurate. For example, if you currently earn $50,000, are there people who earn $100,000 yet they work only 40 hours a week? And are there people who work more than 40 hours a week and earn less than you do?

In my speeches I often ask the audience, "Who wants to win some money?" After everyone in the audience puts up their hands, I call two people onstage. I hand one a picture of a diamond and tell him or her, "Go outside and bring me back all the diamonds you can find lying on the ground." I hand the other person a picture of a rock and say, "Bring me back all the rocks you can find." Then I tell both of them, "Whoever comes back with more diamonds or rocks will get a $100 bill." At this point the audience is laughing—and confused. "Diamonds are so expensive because they're harder to find," I say. "You put 40 rocks in a pile and they're not going to be worth much. But if you put 40 diamonds in a pile, that represents a lot of money. It's the same with the time you spend at work: if you're considered a 'diamond' employee, or your business offers a 'diamond' product or service, your 40 hours a week is going to be worth a lot more. Here's my point: your job as an employee or a business is to figure out how to become as valuable as a diamond."

In order to double your income, you don't need to work double the hours; perhaps you can make more money simply by changing jobs, or getting promoted, or focusing on improving your strengths, or studying a new skill that would make your time and effort more valuable. However, most of us don't think this way. Our beliefs about what it will take to make more income have locked us into a certain way of thinking. Once those beliefs are questioned, however, and once we understand that we can maximize our returns on the efforts we make, then a new world of possibilities opens before us.

#4—Fear of Risk: Hiding Rather than Investing Money

Recently I read a story of a woman in Israel who wanted to do something nice for her elderly mother, so she bought her a mattress and had it delivered to her mother's house. The deliverymen put the new mattress on the bed and threw the old one on the street for the trash collectors. When the woman's mother came home, the daughter proudly showed her the new mattress—and her mother almost fainted. Mom had kept her life savings in the mattress, the equivalent of over $1 million in cash! The daughter rushed to the street but the trash truck had come and gone. The daughter was left searching through the landfill, looking for her mother's money.

The primary reason that people stash their cash instead of taking advantage of Certificates of Deposit, stocks, bonds, mutual funds and so on, is a *lack of information and education about finances*. Even if they're good at managing, saving, and budgeting their income, some individuals are afraid to put their hard-earned savings into even the simplest of investments, especially if they've ever lost a lot of value in their retirement plans or in their home. So rather than taking the time to learn about investing, they go to the local bank and open up a checking or savings account that pays almost no interest, because they know that they can walk in the bank and get their money anytime.

If you lost a lot of value in your retirement plan in the past few years, the piddly bit of interest you earned in your savings account probably looked pretty good. However, if you want to build wealth and financial security, "hiding" your money in this way will never get you the returns you need. Why? One reason is that the interest on most savings accounts doesn't even keep up with inflation—and therefore, your hard-earned money is actually *losing* value. Here's what I mean: if you invested $1,000 10 years ago in a savings account paying 2 percent interest per year, by today you'd have $1,219. But over the same period, suppose that inflation averaged 2.57 percent annually. So every year your money actually *lost* 0.57 percent in value.

Now, there's nothing wrong with using savings accounts and interest-bearing checking to keep emergency fund money. But in the long run, in order to build wealth for retirement and other uses, you'll need to look at other investment choices. And you will need to learn to understand, accept, and manage risk. The good news is that you can learn to use risk to your advantage. For example, if you're 30 years old and investing for retirement, you can take a little more risk because you have a longer time to make up for any losses you might take. But the best way to lessen the "risk of risk" is to invest your money in different things—in other words, to diversify. You'll hear more about this important principle later.

#5—Relying on Friends and Family for Advice Instead of Talking to Experts

I once knew a very successful athlete who was making a lot of money and wanted some advice about what to do with it. The young man's father had a friend who owned a successful car dealership. This man knew a lot about building and running his business—but he knew nothing about investing. Unfortunately, the young man went to his father's friend for advice instead of going to a professional financial adviser, and he lost a lot of money as a result.

There's a very wise saying, "Tell me who you hang out with and I'll tell you who you are." Nowhere is this truer than in your financial life. Tell me who you consult about your finances, and without knowing anything else about you I can tell you what kind of financial life you have. Now, most of us rely on advisers we know, even if that person is not an expert in the area in which we need advice. We go to a tax preparer that does a great job with our taxes and ask him how to invest our refund. Or we have an insurance agent who got us a great deal on auto and homeowner's insurance, so when the agent brings up the mutual funds that his company sells, we buy it simply because we trust him.

If you were buying a house, you'd go to a real estate agent who has experience in the area where you wish to live. However, if you needed someone to do your taxes or prepare the accounting for your business, no matter how good your real estate agent was, he or she wouldn't be an appropriate adviser for those particular jobs. You must be smart about choosing your advisers. Find experts in the areas where you need help, and ask them for advice only in their specialty. To find the best adviser, you must do three things. First, decide what kind of advice you need—investments, real estate, taxes, financial planning, and so on. Second, do your research on people who offer that kind of advice. Check out what I call the three C's: *character, competence,* and *credentials.* And third, meet with the person and check references before you agree to use the services of any professional.

Can you ask for referrals from people you know? Of course. But remember, their situation may be very different from yours, and while they may have a great relationship with this particular financial professional, you may or may not "mesh" in the same way. It's also possible that the person who referred you doesn't know that this adviser isn't providing them with the best advice. In chapter 6 you'll learn some basic guidelines for finding, evaluating, and using the best advisers.

#6—Letting Ego, Embarrassment, or Pride Stop You from Asking Questions or Getting Good Advice

A while ago, my good friend David came to see me to talk about his finances. David confided that even though he had earned a lot of money as a realtor, he had no savings, no estate plan, no money saved for his daughter's education, and very little in his retirement accounts. Now the economic downturn was affecting his real estate business so much that he was afraid of losing his home. He told me that he felt enormous shame, guilt, and embarrassment about his situation. Confessing his financial state of affairs to me was the most difficult thing he had ever done because it hurt his pride as a man. Even though David knew that I was an expert in personal finances, he didn't want to tell me about his difficulties. David was caught in the trap of ego, embarrassment, and pride. He was proud of his identity as a "successful" realtor, and he didn't want to admit his financial woes to anybody.

Even those of us who aren't in difficult circumstances financially can let ego, embarrassment, or pride stop us from asking the important questions or seeking the help we need. Many people would even rather be ripped off than embarrassed. For example, once a young woman consulted me about retirement planning, and I noticed she had a rather expensive annuity policy. When I asked her about it, she got very defensive. "I bought it five years ago, right after my divorce," she said. "The man at my bank said it would provide me with guaranteed income when I retire." I pointed out to her that she was still in her early thirties—a long way from retirement—and the money she paid for that annuity every month probably could be invested in many other ways that would provide her with greater returns and a larger nest egg when she did reach 65. "I can't go back to the bank and tell them I made a mistake," she replied stubbornly. "I'd look like an idiot." This woman was prepared to take a financial hit of tens of thousands of dollars over the course of her life just because she didn't want to look like an idiot in front of a financial services salesperson.

All too often we fail to ask important questions because we don't want to look stupid. Instead, when we purchase something on credit, or we have to sign a multi-page contract, we glance over it as if we understood every word, ask a couple of simple questions, and then sign and trust that what we've been told is true. But here's the truth: Most people are intimidated by legal and financial language. For example, if you have mutual funds as part of your retirement plan, did you ever actually *read* the fund prospectus? Or if you've purchased a property and it's gone to escrow, did you wade through the agreement, reading it line by line and asking questions about anything you didn't understand? (Here in California any property purchase involves about 60 pages of documents filled with legal and financial language, and the buyer is supposed to sign and initial almost every page. How many people do you think actually read each page?)

Unfortunately, in the U.S. we've seen very clearly how people got into serious financial difficulty because they didn't understand their mortgages or the buyer's agreements. Worse still, because of ego, embarrassment, or pride, many people keep quiet and never try to do anything about even the most unfair contracts. However, the worst thing you can do is to keep quiet. If you believe you have been cheated or treated unfairly, go to a trusted adviser and ask what you should do. There are local, state, and federal organizations that oversee almost every kind of business and profession, and they all have formal complaint programs. If the issue is important enough, you may wish to consult an attorney to see if you can take any action legally, either through small claims or other civil courts. But don't let ego, embarrassment, or pride keep you from fighting for your rights as a customer and consumer. And don't allow the same emotions to keep you from doing whatever is necessary to understand contracts and get the best financial advice in the first place.

#7 — Scarcity and Abundance: A Slice of Pie, or a Pie Shop?

Do you feel that there's enough to go around for everyone? Or is life a "dog eat dog" fight for survival? Your beliefs about scarcity and abundance have a significant effect on your relationship with money. Scarcity means if you win, I lose. If my competitor's business is doing well, mine will suffer as a result, so I'll do whatever's necessary to take market share away from them. Scarcity thinking views life like a pie in a world of very hungry people: there's only so much pie to go around, and once the pie is gone, it's gone. If you take a big piece, then that means there's less for the rest of us. If you think of life like that, no wonder you get angry when you see someone who has more "pie" than you do, and do your best to make sure they don't take any more!

However, I believe in living in abundance, where there's more than enough to go around. We don't have to compete for a "piece of the pie" because there's a universal "pie shop" creating more pies all the time. In an abundant world, if I win, you win, too. There will always be enough for anyone who is willing to work for it, and if I'm successful, it can open the doors for you to be successful as well. Most wealthy people never spend time worrying about who's got the biggest piece of pie because they're busy creating more businesses and more abundance. When you believe there is always going to be more than enough, then it doesn't matter if your brother-in-law buys an expensive car, or a competitor opens an office in your neighborhood, or your friend moves into a bigger house. You know that there always will be plenty of wealth to go around.

The best way to step out of scarcity and into abundance and success is gratitude. Be grateful for what you have. Instead of looking at someone else and saying, "Why am I struggling when they're doing so well?" take a moment to appreciate the gifts you already possess: life, health, family and friends. Know that abundance is all around us and that you can access it with your efforts. When we focus on gratitude and abundance and believe there's more than enough to go around, we take charge of creating our own abundance. All it takes is a little skill, a little patience, a little hard work—and a willingness to build our own "pie shop."

#8—The Lotto Mentality: Believing You Can Get Something for Nothing

Not far from my office, there's a convenience store where I occasionally stop for a cup of coffee. One afternoon I noticed a long line in front of the counter. "What's going on?" I asked a woman in line. "The Super Lotto jackpot is up to $79 million this week," she said excitedly. "I'm buying tickets for my whole family!" Another friend of mine plays the Lotto each week with his colleagues at work. "One day we'll win and we can all retire," he explained. Everyone knows that expecting to finance retirement this way is never going to work. But this is an example of the "lotto mentality": believing that you can get something for nothing.

The "lotto mentality" appears in many forms other than a lottery ticket. A friend says, "My sister got a hot stock tip from someone who works for XYZ Company. If you buy their stock, you'll make a killing." Or someone tells you, "You need your house rewired? My brother knows how to do it. He's not licensed, but it'll cost you half of what you'd pay for an electrician." Of course, when you lose your shirt on the hot stock, or your house burns down because of the brother's shoddy work, you're stuck. If you want to do or build something worthwhile, you have to be willing to put in time, work, and sometimes money. A farmer has to put in the hard work of planting, weeding, fertilizing, watering every day if he wants to reap a sizable harvest. If you think you can get around putting in the work, in the short term you may be able to get away with it, sure—but laziness and sloppiness will always come back to haunt you.

Behind the lotto mentality is greed, which causes people to make mistakes, take shortcuts, and get suckered into all kinds of "get-rich-quick" schemes and scams. If there's one lesson we should have learned over the past few years, it's that there is no such thing as "instant" money. As I remind people, "God makes the fish and God makes the nets, but God doesn't put fish *in* the nets. God helps those who help themselves." I believe we need to make the most of our hard-earned money for ourselves and our families. That means being willing to put in the work first, and then be smart about where we invest our resources. Remember: when it sounds too good to be true, it usually is.

#9—Procrastination: The Thief of Time and Money

Imagine yourself on the day you turn 62, or 65, or whatever age you've set in your mind to retire. You're ready to take it easy and to do the things you never had time for when you were working. But somehow you never managed to save much over the years. You put little to nothing into the retirement account plans offered by your employer. Whenever you had a little extra money, instead of opening an IRA you spent it on vacations, or buying the latest gadget, or other things that seemed more important at the time. You thought, "Next year, when I'm making more money, I'll put it away for retirement"—but every year that money always got spent on other things. Now, at the age when you hoped to retire, you look at your bank balance and realize there's no way you can make ends meet with your Social Security and the little bit you have saved. You either need to move in with relatives or take a part-time job until you get too old or sick to work. Procrastination, the thief of time and money, has stolen the retirement you always wanted.

As someone once wrote, procrastinators are living in "Someday Isle," the island of unfulfilled dreams. There, everyone walks around saying things like, "Someday I'll start my own business." "Someday I'll spend the weekend with my kids." "Someday I'll go on that second honeymoon." "Someday I'll put away money for retirement." But "someday" never comes, and all they have left are a bunch of empty promises and painful thoughts of what might have been.

I realize that it's all too easy to get caught up in the needs of the moment without ever looking a few years down the road. And many people feel they are just barely keeping their heads above water dealing with the urgent stuff. "I have to get the car fixed," they'll tell me. "I can't put money away this month. I'll do it next month." Their intentions are always good, but you know where the road paved with good intentions ends up. I once heard a pastor say, "If the devil doesn't make you bad, he makes you busy." There's nothing wrong with dealing with things that are urgent; however, focusing on the urgent stuff means that most of us never get around to the things that are far more important—like spending time with our kids when they're growing up. Like keeping our relationships with our spouses strong. Like saving for retirement early and investing consistently through the years.

Every day you put off doing what's important is a day that is lost forever. And at the end of your life, those lost days will be some of your biggest regrets. You have to keep one eye on the present and one on the future. For example, if you delay putting money aside to fund your children's education, then you and your kids may suffer the pain of not having the funds for them to go to college. The time to start a child's college fund is the day that child is born. All of us know that we will need to save for the future, whether it be to take care of emergencies, cover our basic needs when we retire, or just to have a little "walking-around" money when we're old. But the time to put that money aside is now, not later—today, not tomorrow. Because tomorrow comes sooner than we think, and it costs a lot more than we want it to.

Another problem that arises with procrastination is what I call the "why bother" syndrome. People tell me, "Why should I save for my child's college education? No one in my family has ever gone to college." Or, "Why should I save for retirement? I put money aside and it just disappeared in the recession. When it's time to retire I'll get Social Security, and I may have to move in with my kids, but I can't see any reason to keep pouring money into retirement accounts that just disappear." Certainly factors other than procrastination can affect our finances and our future. Maybe you did save for retirement consistently, only to see your accounts shrink in recent years. And maybe you're frustrated because you feel circumstances have undermined your efforts. But that doesn't mean you should give up. If you go through a tough patch, it's even more important to pick yourself up and start saving again immediately (hopefully, wiser for the losses you have experienced). If you cannot see the light at the end of the tunnel today, believe that it is still there—but only if you avoid the thief, procrastination, and start saving again now.

Let's imagine once more that you are getting ready to retire, only through the years you have saved as much as possible. You put your money into a variety of investments and kept track of how they have fared. You have a very clear plan for how your retirement years will be funded, not spending everything at once but taking care of yourself well no matter how long you live. You have enough for your basic needs and a few luxuries, like travel or gifts for your children or grandchildren. You won't need to work to make ends meet. You look forward to a long and happy retirement. How great does this version feel?

Long-term thinking, begun *today*, will help you create the future of your dreams. After all, our lives unfold so quickly.... We start work, blink, and all of a sudden we're meeting with HR to discuss retirement options. We get married, and the next thing we know, kids appear. In another blink of an eye they're graduating, going off to college or work, and getting married. The tomorrow we thought we had plenty of time to prepare for suddenly is next week, or next month, or even the next minute. That's why we need a dual vision: one eye on the present, the other on the future. Every day that you wait you lose a little more of the power of time to help you create the life you want. Let time be your ally. Instead of "tomorrow," say "today."

Three Simple Steps to Change Limiting Beliefs

Getting rid of limiting or negative beliefs is so simple, yet most of us believe it's difficult or impossible. But remember: most of our beliefs are things that we make up, or that we've heard from other people. We have never tested them, and in fact, we don't know whether they are true or not. Luckily, changing a belief is relatively simple. All it takes is awareness and openness to discovering the truth that will set you free.

Step One: Make a list of any negative beliefs about money and finances.

Start by looking at your financial life to date. Are you making the kind of money you'd like? Are you experiencing the kind of abundance you and your family deserve? If not, what beliefs are holding you back? Make a list of every negative belief you have around money and finances. Use the beliefs listed in this chapter as examples. Do you have conflicting beliefs about money being good or bad? Do you believe it's someone else's job to take care of your finances? Do you feel that investing is too risky? Do you choose advisers just because you like them and follow their advice without checking it? Have you ever let ego or embarrassment stop you from asking questions or kept you from revealing a financial mistake? Do you fear there's not enough to go around? Have you ever tried to cut corners and get something for nothing? Have you postponed saving or investing or doing anything truly important, telling yourself that you'll do it tomorrow?

Be completely honest, even though you might be surprised at what shows up on your list. Remember, these are simply beliefs that you adopted somewhere along the line, and they can be changed if they do not serve you.

Once you have your list, for each belief ask yourself, "How is this belief working for me? Has it brought me what I want? What results have I created with this belief?" If the results aren't what you want, then it's time to make a few changes.

Step Two: Look at each belief and ask, "How is this not true?"

Come up with examples from your own life that show these beliefs up for what they are—lies that are holding you back. If your belief is, "I'm not good with money," when have you handled money well and responsibly? If you think, "I can never save enough for retirement," was there a time when you put aside money for anything—a bicycle or a concert ticket when you were a kid, for instance? If you can't come up with examples from your own life, think of examples from other people's lives. If you believe that only sophisticated people can make money on their investments, think of people like UPS drivers or teachers, who made very little each year yet were able to leave millions of dollars to charity when they passed away. Find examples of ways your old, negative beliefs about money, abundance, and so on, aren't true.

Step Three: For every negative belief, come up with a positive belief to take its place.

Now comes the fun part! You get to *choose* what you want to believe. If you believe money is the root of all evil, what would be the truth? Perhaps something like, "Money allows me to do good at a much higher level." (And by the way, the Bible actually says the *love* of money is the root of evil, not money itself.) If your belief is "I'm not good with money," maybe all you need is a little more education, confidence, and good advice. For each belief on your list, write down a positive belief that would help you create more happiness and abundance. Once you have your new beliefs, keep reading them over while you ask, "*How* is this true?" The more certain you feel about a new belief, the easier it will be for you to incorporate it into your life.

Whatever your current address on My Street, you've arrived there because of your beliefs. If your address on My Street isn't where you want it to be, you can start the process of change by changing your beliefs. But you can't keep believing and doing the same things over and over and make a lot of progress. As Albert Einstein once said, the definition of insanity is doing the same thing over and over and expecting different results. To change your results, you have to change both your beliefs and actions, and through the years I've discovered that changing beliefs must come first. The choices you make about your beliefs may shape your financial future for good or ill. Get rid of negative beliefs, and you'll find that the move from your current street to a much better neighborhood will be smoother, faster, and a lot more enjoyable.

The Heart of the Matter

Nine beliefs that may be holding you back:

➤ #1: Conflicting beliefs about money

➤ #2: Depending on others to take care of you

➤ #3: Effort versus reward: working harder isn't necessarily the answer

➤ #4: Fear of risk: hiding rather than investing money

➤ #5: Relying on friends and family for advice instead of talking to experts

➤ #6: Letting ego, embarrassment, or pride stop you from asking questions or getting good advice

➤ #7: Scarcity and abundance: a slice of pie, or a pie shop?

➤ #8: The Lotto mentality: believing you can get something for nothing

➤ #9: Procrastination: the thief of time and money

➤ There are three simple steps to change a limiting or negative belief: make a list of your negative beliefs, come up with ways these beliefs are not true (examples from your own life or the lives of others), and create positive beliefs to substitute for the old negative beliefs.

PART

2

**Creating Success and Happiness
on My Street**

It's easy to create success and feel happy in good times—but nothing is forever. Good times inevitably are followed by challenges. Whether those challenges and problems are personal or affect everyone, we need to do what we can, when we can, to prepare for bad times before they arrive. It's like the old fable of the ant and the grasshopper. The ant works hard all summer to store up food while the grasshopper plays. Come winter, the ant lives on what it put aside, but the grasshopper has nothing.

However, what if the ant has worked hard to put aside "food," i.e., money, only to find its stores wiped out by a fire, or flood, or someone (or something—like a recession) stepping on its anthill? Imagine the poor ant standing outside the ruin of its home, all of its stores gone, and along comes the grasshopper. "Tough luck," it says with a smile. "It's a shame—you worked so hard for so long, and it got you nothing. At least I enjoyed the good times while they lasted!"

However, I imagine that the ant would look at the grasshopper and shake its head. "I may have lost what I saved, but I know how to build it up again," the ant would say. "The same habits that got me to where I was will help me and my family to survive this setback." And the ant would head back out and start accumulating food once more.

The best thing we can do in good and bad times is to develop the *habits of success*: things like hard work, persistence, vision, planning, patience, ongoing evaluation, and yes, gratitude and giving back. Old-fashioned principles, yes—but there's a reason that such traits are consistently rewarded: they make us better human beings while they help us create a brighter future for our families and ourselves. When we work to develop the habits of success, we can succeed when things outside our control are doing well, and we can cope when things outside our control are difficult.

Let me give you a couple of examples. Let's say you run five miles a day, rain or shine. When you first started training, it wasn't easy because you hadn't built the habit of running. Maybe you ran a mile and stopped because your feet hurt. Maybe you looked outside the window, saw it was pouring rain, and decided to stay inside. It took you at least a couple of months until you built the habit of running. If you were persistent and managed to do enough daily runs, eventually you would run no matter what. When the weather was perfect and your feet and legs felt great, you ran a little further, or a little faster. When the weather was terrible, or your feet were bothering you, you still ran—and you're no longer as affected by adverse conditions. You kept running because that's what you do. You've built a habit of success that supports you.

Now, imagine you're a young person going to work for the very first time. Your parents say, "Make sure you put aside 10 percent of your paycheck every week for the future." You save that 10 percent every week and set up a long-term plan to ensure your financial stability. For 10 years, the nest egg grows very well, and by the time you are ready to get married and start a family, your money has doubled. Your investments provided good returns, yes; but more important, you've continued to save 10 percent of your income every week. But at this point, the market crashes. The value of your nest egg drops by 50 percent. The economy turns sour, and you lose your job. However, through the years you have built the habits of prudent spending, of investing carefully, and of always looking ahead. You have a contingency plan in place and some money saved. Instead of sitting and complaining about the economy, or continuing to go after the same kind of job you lost, maybe you volunteer at a local nonprofit, or take classes to improve your job skills. You keep your spirits up by spending time with your friends and family. You attend church or follow some kind of meaningful spiritual practice. You exercise both your body and mind. With all of these habits of success, you weather the downturn. Eventually you find a job that's right for you, and you begin saving 10 percent of your income once again.

The easiest way to develop the habits of success is to *pursue goals that are important to you.* Why would a runner go out daily, rain or shine, unless he or she had a goal they were pursuing? That goal might be to lose weight, or to improve their health, or to build lean, strong, runner's muscles. Perhaps they've always wanted to run a marathon, or they have certain health issues they need to overcome, or perhaps they're dating someone who is a runner and they want to share the experience. In the same way, people put money aside not because they want to deprive themselves today, but because they have a goal of being able to live securely when they retire.

It's said that success is a journey rather than a destination; however, I've found that we still need signposts along the way to let us know if we're on the right road and to tell us how far we've come. Goals are those signposts. They let us know how we're doing, how far we've come, and how far we still have to go. They give us a chance to celebrate our wins and then build upon them for greater success. Goals help us take a task that can seem overwhelming and break it into more manageable sections. They create the confidence we need to keep moving ahead. However, statistics show that few people take the time to decide upon their goals and create a plan to reach them. Instead, we find ourselves drifting through life, reacting to events rather than responding to them resourcefully. We live like grasshoppers instead of ants—partying when the times are good and going through a lot of pain when things get tough.

Luckily, most of the people that I meet every day—the ones that live on My Street—aren't afraid of hard work. They're willing to build the habits of success so they and their families can live better lives. I developed the Confidence Cycle to help just those people. It's a six-step program that will help you choose and achieve important goals while you build the habits that will make you more secure, happier, and more successful in every area. Each of the steps of the cycle builds upon the one before it, leading you systematically to your goals.

Here's what the Confidence Cycle looks like:

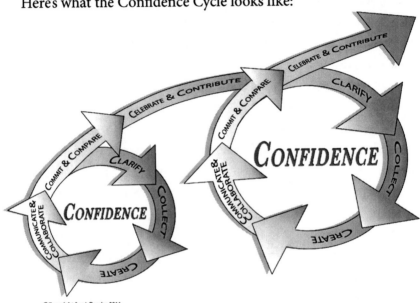

©Copyright LouisBarajas 2011

You'll see that the Confidence Cycle is literally an upward spiral. With each goal you work towards, with each habit of success that you develop, you'll find yourself moving higher and higher. Your goals will become greater, as will your self-confidence. There will be setbacks and challenges, of course; but you'll find yourself overcoming them far more easily than you might have thought possible. Eventually you'll look back at where you started and be amazed at the progress you've made and who you've become as a result. It's a great feeling, and one that you deserve to experience.

The next few chapters will explain each step of the Confidence Cycle. There are exercises that will help you put these steps into action. You'll find examples of ways to use these steps to develop greater levels of financial confidence as well as creating great things in other areas of your life. Follow these steps, and you'll be amazed at how quickly you achieve results you only dreamed of before—or perhaps you never even had the courage to envision.

Staying on T.R.A.C. with the Confidence Cycle

In order to build true and lasting confidence, however, you must begin with four principles that I consider the *cornerstones of success*: Truth, Responsibility, Awareness, and Courage. In the same way that a building needs a foundation with four strong cornerstones if it is to last, you need these four principles as a foundation before you start pursuing your goals. When you adopt these principles and live them daily, you'll stay on T.R.A.C. as you build (or rebuild) the confidence you need to live happily on My Street.

Cornerstone #1: TRUTH

Sometimes the most difficult person to tell the truth to is yourself. We all have a certain self-image that we need to preserve in order to feel good. If something contradicts that self-image, we usually do our best to deny it, ignore it, or delay dealing with it. However, we've all seen the effects of not telling the truth about where we are and where we need to be, both as a society and as individuals. Many of us are in trouble because we weren't told the truth about our investments, or what we could afford to purchase given our income levels. We didn't look carefully at the possible consequences of our financial habits, and we also suffered from the lies and missteps of businesses and governments. And now we're suffering the consequences of this general lack of honesty.

Now, there may not be a lot we can do about honesty in our corporations and governments, but we *can* tell the truth about ourselves. To create a secure future for yourself and your family, you need to be painfully honest with yourself about everything—your motives, resources, timeline, expectations, fears, and knowledge. In each step of the Confidence Cycle, make a point to be honest about your current situation as well as your resources. Starting with a clear and truthful picture of where you are today will make it easier to build your confidence from this point forward.

Cornerstone #2: RESPONSIBILITY

There's a story about a man on his deathbed. He says to his wife, "Honey, you've always been there for me. You were with me when I lost my job. You were with me when I burned the house down accidentally. You were with me when my back went out and I couldn't walk for six months. You were with me when our daughter married the Hell's Angel. You were with me when she left him and moved back in with her three kids. You've been with me through some of the toughest times a man could experience." After a moment he adds, "Maybe *you're* the one that brought me all the bad luck!"

Too often when faced with challenges our first response is to look around for someone or something to blame. Of course, circumstances beyond our control can affect our goals. If our child gets sick, it can derail our plans for a romantic vacation with a spouse. When the company goes bankrupt, everyone loses their jobs. When the real estate market in your area drops by 30 or 50 percent, your home value also may go down. However, the only way to build confidence is to take responsibility for your life and your actions. You may not be able to take the vacation with your spouse, but the two of you might be able to sneak away for lunch. You can't prevent your company from closing, but you can build a strong network of contacts in case you need to find another job. You may not be able to do anything about the fact that the value of your home has gone down, but you can pay your mortgage on time and keep your property in good shape so that when values go up again (as they eventually will), the value of your house is likely to rise with the neighborhood.

A great man once described personal responsibility as a formula: the *events* of our lives, plus our *response* to those events, create the *outcomes* we experience. We may not control events, but we always can control our response to those events. For example, two different people might be faced with tax bills they're unable to pay. Person A responds by freaking out, blaming their accountant, or the government, or their spouse and kids who spend too much, and then delaying doing anything about the bill until he gets multiple notices from the IRS. Eventually the IRS will come after him for the tax bill and penalties. Person B, on the other hand, responds to the notice by reviewing his tax return with his accountant to make sure there was no mistake on his part or the part of the IRS, and then he contacts the IRS to arrange a payment plan to cover the additional tax bill. He also makes sure to adjust his withholding and review his taxes so that such a problem never happens again. The same circumstances with two different responses lead to two different outcomes.

Circumstances do not have to dictate the road of our lives; they merely show us that we need to change the paths we take to get to our destination. While you can't control most events, you *can* control your thoughts, attitudes, choices, and decisions. Only when you take responsibility for your life can you actually do something to make things better. You must adopt the belief, "Regardless of circumstances, I am responsible for my future."

Cornerstone #3: AWARENESS

Awareness is different from telling the truth. With truth, you face the hard facts you know but you're uncomfortable with. In awareness, you are noticing things that have never even been on your radar before. You can't change what you don't acknowledge, and if you can't see the problem, then how can you acknowledge it and change it?

Many of us have a limited awareness of all of the different aspects of our lives. For example, do you really know how strong your relationship is with your spouse and your children? Do you have a clear picture of your career track and what you need to do to earn more, get promoted, or build your business? Are you aware financially of how much you spend, how much you save, and how much you'll need for retirement? Do you know how healthy you are?

To build confidence in any area, you have to be aware of the places where you don't have the information you need or where you may lack the education to make good choices. Simply by reading this book you have taken the first important step in developing awareness. When you move through the Confidence Cycle, you will gain both the knowledge and awareness that will help you ask better questions and make better choices when it comes to your finances and your life.

Cornerstone #4: COURAGE

Truth, responsibility, and awareness will show you what to do, but it will take courage to go and do it. For most people, taking action can be difficult and frightening. They're afraid to make a mistake, or to make *another* mistake. However, the only way to build confidence is to have the courage to take action, learn from your mistakes, and then take action again. Think of it as learning to play an instrument, or a sport. You learn, practice, learn more, practice, and then learn more. With each lesson and practice you build confidence in yourself and your abilities. It's the same with gaining confidence and building the habits of success. You learn, put what you have learned into practice, and then you learn from your results. You put these new lessons into practice, learn more, and the cycle continues. But only if you have the courage to learn and practice will you gain the benefits of your efforts.

As Ambrose Redmoon wrote, "Courage is not the absence of fear, but the judgment that something else is more important than fear." Courage is doing what you know you need to do in spite of the fear you feel. When you tell the truth to yourself, take responsibility for your response to circumstances (instead of letting yourself be controlled by them), and have the courage to learn, try, learn, and try again, then you will be able to build your confidence and create a better future for you and your family on My Street.

The Heart of the Matter

➤ To take care of yourself and your family in both good and bad times, you must develop the habits of success: things like hard work, persistence, vision, planning, patience, gratitude, and giving back.

➤ The easiest way to adopt the habits of success is to pursue goals that are important to you. When you do so, you enter the Confidence Cycle, a six-step program that will help you become more secure, happier, and successful.

➤ Underpin your confidence and goals with the four cornerstones of success: truth, responsibility, awareness, and courage.

3

Step 1: Clarify
Get a Picture of the Life You Want

In *Small Business, Big Life*, I told a story of a man receiving a lifetime achievement award in his community. When he got up to give his acceptance speech, you could see something was bothering him. He thanked his family for putting up with his relentless focus on business. "I missed a lot of date nights, soccer practices, school plays, and family vacations, but I hope you think it was worth it," he said with tears in his eyes. However, only his wife had bothered to come to the award ceremony. The man's two grown daughters never felt much connection with their father; they knew he had always put his business first, so they didn't care to see him get the award.

All of us find ourselves riding the day-to-day train of life. We keep traveling on the tracks in front of us, riding from station to station, never thinking that maybe we should stop, get off the train, and take a look at the route so we can see if we like the track we're on. Instead, we stay on the train of life as it whizzes along. Before we know it, our small children are grown-ups. We've lost all our hair or gained a set of love handles. We've spent 20, 30, 40 years on the job. We're celebrating our 20th wedding anniversary but there's no passion in our relationship. Our days are almost done and we're wondering where the time went.

Certainly finances and work need to be a focus of our lives, but as someone once reminded me, "You never see a U-Haul behind a hearse." Money, wealth, possessions, success are *means* to an end than ends in themselves. Most of us on My Street know this already. We don't want a Rolls-Royce; we just want to live better lives with dignity. We want to take care of our families, spend time with our children and grandchildren, and live free from fear about the future. We understand that real happiness comes from good health, good relationships, fulfilling work that pays well enough for us to take care of our families, loving and being loved by others, and a sense of purpose and meaning. But we don't think that we can actually create a *plan* that will help us live that kind of fulfilling life.

I'm here to tell you that it's possible to choose how you travel on the journey of life. The first step is to look at the big picture, to *clarify* what's important to you, and then to create a plan to ensure you have more of that in your life. If you plan your future now, you are far more likely to create the life you truly want for yourself and your family.

The Big Picture: What Do You Want Your Life to Be About?

Because I speak about personal finance, when people talk to me about their ideal future they'll usually say things like, "Ten years from now I'd like to have $500,000 saved for retirement."

"Great!" I'll tell them. "Sell your house and rent a room for you and your family to live in. Eat only beans and rice, never buy anything, live on 10 percent of your salary and put the other 90 percent into the bank. If you do that you'll be well on your way to your goal of $500,000 in 10 years."

At this point they look at me like I'm crazy. "I'm not going to do that!" they say. "That's no way for my family to live."

"Of course not," I respond. "What you really want is not a particular amount of money in the bank, but to be able to create a certain quality of life for you and your family. You need to be clear on that lifestyle first. Only then can you determine the part that money will play in supporting that goal."

Planning for your financial future without knowing the big picture of the life you want is like trying to put together a jigsaw puzzle where you can't see the picture on the box. You have a lot of pieces scattered on the table, but you're blindly trying to put them together with no guide for where they go or how they fit. When you spend a little time on life planning, you can figure out how the different elements of your finances, career, time, and energy can fit together to give you and your family the best quality of life.

Recently a good friend came to me with a dilemma. She had been nominated for a high-level position in the federal government in Washington, D.C. It was her dream job, but there was one huge catch: the job paid one-third less than she was currently earning. "Louis, I can't afford that kind of a pay cut," she told me. "It wouldn't be fair to my family to have to change our standard of living that much."

"Remember when we first met almost 20 years ago?" I asked. "You were a teacher, and you told me that you had gone into education because all you wanted to do was to help children learn and grow. Will this job let you do that?"

"Absolutely," she answered. "It's the opportunity of a lifetime. I'd be able to help kids all across the country."

"If that's so, then let's see how we can make that opportunity a reality," I said. We spent the next six months creating a plan so that she and her family could live well on the lower salary. They reduced expenses, rented out their home in California, and made some adjustments to their investments. It took a lot of sacrifice and hard work, but she accepted the job, and everyone is truly happy that she did.

The first step in building confidence is getting your life priorities straight. Your vision of a great life may have nothing to do with money but everything to do with spending time with your kids, or providing a happy home for your aging parents, or contributing time to a charity or social cause that's dear to your heart, or simply having some leisure time to spend with your spouse. But when you finally see the "big picture" of how you can be fulfilled in many different areas of your life, you'll be surprised at the relief you experience.

You start to believe that it's possible to live a life filled with happiness instead of stress. You'll be excited and committed, ready to create a plan to achieve your ideal life and then put it into action. And over the months you'll discover the delight of watching your *real* dreams come true.

However, even when you have a picture of the life you want to create, you need to understand why. In truth, most of us don't make the time to reflect and discover what's truly important to us. Instead, we set what I call "politically correct" financial goals—things we're told we should want, like a certain amount saved for retirement, owning a home, putting money aside for your children's education, and so on. While these are admirable goals, unless you know why you want them you're unlikely to put in the work needed to achieve them. This is true especially when life happens—you lose a job, or there's an unexpected illness, or a new baby is on the way. At that point your goals go out the window because they were weak to begin with. And weak goals are nothing more than New Year's resolutions: made quickly, and abandoned just as quickly when they become inconvenient.

Luckily, there is a power inside us that can help us strengthen our resolve from this point forward. It's the power of our own individual reasons for action. Once you know why you want to succeed, and those reasons are exciting to you, then everything else falls into place. Discovering your whys is the first step of building confidence. Now, you still have to take action consistently in order to create consistent results. But when you have good, strong, personal reasons for taking action, then it's a lot easier to get out of bed each morning and create the life of your dreams.

Create the Vision for Your Ideal Life

Imagine you had a magic wand that you could wave to make things perfect. What would your ideal future be like? Where do you want to live? What's your lifestyle? Where would you work? What would your children be like? What kind of home would you have? What activities would you enjoy? Describe everything that you'd want in your perfect life; paint the picture for yourself. The journey to the life you want begins with vision, and the key to an effective life vision is clarity. Once you're clear on your vision—your "big picture"—then you can create a plan that will help you get wherever you want to go.

An effective life vision must include three key elements: (1) your *life focus areas*, the areas of your life in which you put the most effort and attention—for example, family, work, finances, and so on. Once you've identified those, you need to know (2) the feelings and emotions you *value* and want to experience on a regular basis. These values are your "whys" for doing what you do. When you are clear on your values, you can set (3) the *goals* that will help you have more of those feelings and experience more fulfillment in your life focus areas. In this chapter you'll clarify all three elements of your vision. This process will help you focus your efforts and produce greater results much faster. (I recommend you get a journal or some kind of notebook where you can write your answers to the questions in the rest of this book.)

1. Clarify Your *Life Focus Areas*

Your major *life focus areas* are the parts of your life that need attention. When all of these areas are in alignment, you feel successful and have greater peace of mind. When they're out of alignment, you end up constantly busy but with no sense of fulfillment. And if you don't take care and nurture certain major areas—like your health or your relationships—your whole life becomes difficult and unfulfilling.

I have noticed that there are 10 areas of life most people say that they need to focus on in order to be happy. Here they are, in no particular order:

» Physical (health and fitness)

» Intellectual

» Spiritual

» Relationships

» Recreational (fun)

» Professional (work/career)

» Personal Growth

» Material (possessions)

» Charitable

» Financial

The life areas that are important to you are indicators of your current priorities. If you're newly married, relationships may be your top focus; if you just started a new job after being laid off, finances might be a high priority. Most of us have around four or five as our top focus areas, depending on our current situation. To discover your current life focus areas, ask yourself the following questions.

1. **What are the most important major areas of your life, the areas where you put the most focus?** Refer to the above list as needed.

2. **Are there areas you are over-focusing on right now that are throwing your life out of balance? Are there areas missing that could cause problems later on?** Lots of people pour all their attention and focus into their career or family, and completely forget that other parts of life—health, for example—need to be priorities as well. Even if you have a lot of money 30 years from now, what kind of shape will you be in to enjoy it if you don't take care of your health today? In the same way, if you're putting all your attention on work and no attention on saving for the future, you could definitely experience pain.

3. **What areas do you *need* to work on to feel truly success-ful?** Identify the top three areas of focus that, if you put your efforts there, you would consider your life very fulfilling. What areas would create the greatest impact? However, this doesn't mean you can neglect the other areas you consider important. Your life is like a cosmic workout: to get into great shape, you have to do different exercises for different parts of your body—cardiovascular exercise for your heart, weights for your arms, and so on. Now, some areas may need more work than others, so for a while you spend more time lifting weights, for instance. But to be healthy, you also must keep up your cardiovascular workout. In the same way, each important life focus area needs to receive enough attention to keep it running smoothly.

Creating a great life often means we need to focus on areas that we may be ignoring. Not long ago a gentleman told me that his life focus areas were professional, financial, and relationships. However, I could see that he was at least 100 pounds overweight. "With these life focus areas you stand a good chance of being the most successful, best loved man in the cemetery," I told him. "If you don't take care of your health, you won't be able to accomplish your goals in any other area."

"I never thought of it that way," he replied. "I always figured success in business and taking care of my family were the two most important things in my life, but if I want to be here to enjoy my success, I guess I'd better make my physical health a priority too."

Determining your major focus areas is a great way to look at your life from a broader perspective, and to see all the crucial elements that make up a great life. Knowing your life focus areas will help you set goals that will lead to greater fulfillment on a daily basis.

2. Discover Your *Values*

Everything we do in life, we do in order to get a particular kind of feeling. Do we go to work to make money? Not really. We go to work so we can feel successful, or secure, or for the connection with our colleagues. Our feelings motivate us and make us feel fulfilled or un-fulfilled. They drive our actions and affect our choices about life. The feelings that are important to us—the ones we want to experience the most—we call *values*. We value different feelings in the different areas of our lives. In the area of "profession" or "career," for example, you may value respect, or accomplishment, or success. In the area of relationships, you may list love, intimacy, caring, sharing, and so on.

Everyone's values are unique to him or her. If you value freedom, you may work hard to earn enough so that you can be *free* to go on great vacations and pursue your hobbies. On the other hand, your brother may value security and work hard to put away as much money as he possibly can, so that he'll feel *secure* in his ability to care for himself and his family. Do you think you and your brother would make very different choices because you value different feelings?

And it's not just the value, but *how you define* that value that makes a difference. If you value love, how will you know when you have it? Do you need an adoring spouse and two kids who run to meet you when you come home from work? Or is love something you can feel anytime you give love to someone? If you're wise, you'll find a lot of ways to feel these important emotions in your life every day. When you identify the feelings you value, and discover your definition for those emotions, you'll know (1) the targets you're aiming for and (2) how to "shoot" so you'll hit them more often.

Ask yourself the following questions:

1. **In each of the top three areas of your life, what are the feelings you consider most important to experience regularly?** Make sure you list feelings, not ways to get those feelings. For example, "money" is not an emotion. What *feeling* do you associate with money?

2. **For each feeling/value, how do you know when you have it?** If you value love, what has to happen for you to feel loved? Write down your version of how to experience that particular value.

I once spoke with two business partners who each told me that they valued success. However, when I asked them how they knew they were successful, one partner said, "When we have a steady, reliable stream of income regardless of the economic climate, so we can keep all of our current employees." The other partner answered, "When we are aggressively pursuing new business and taking the kinds of chances that puts us in the forefront of our industry and helps our employees to grow." It's not surprising that these two partners often disagreed about how to run their business! However, both of them also had "taking care of people" high on their values lists, and the way they knew they were taking care of people involved respecting others' values. Because of this, they were able to respect their different perspectives and do well together in their business.

Knowing your values will allow you to make better choices. If you value family, for instance, and you have to choose between a job that will allow you to come home every night versus one that makes you travel five days a week, your choice will be clear. You'd probably even be willing to take a job that paid slightly less if it meant you could be with your family more. Knowing what you value in each of your major life focus areas will help you choose goals that will give you more of those feelings, and thus help you be more fulfilled.

3. Set Powerful and Compelling *Goals*

After identifying your life areas and values, you're ready to set powerful, compelling goals. Interestingly enough, this is the step where most of us start. We say, "I want to save for my kid's education," or "I want to retire at age 65," or "I want to move to a bigger house next year." All very important goals—but if these goals aren't linked to the *reasons* that will truly motivate us, then the chances of achieving those goals are slim. In truth, the best reasons for accomplishing our goals are found in our life focus areas, and values. When we link a goal to a life focus area and value that are important to us, then we're more likely to follow through when the going gets tough.

For example, let's say you set a goal of moving to a bigger house next year. Why do you want to move? You might say, "Well, we need more room," or "The school system's better in this other neighborhood." But what if you consciously looked at your life focus areas and values to discover the reasons this goal should matter? Let's say that one of your most important life focus areas is your family. You were divorced a few years ago, now you've remarried, and you want to create a strong relationship between your new spouse and your children. Your top value is love, and your highest priority is to make sure that your kids as well as your new spouse feel completely loved by you. When you know your top life focus area (relationships) and value (love), you start to realize that there are powerful reasons to find a bigger house. You want a fresh start for your new marriage. You and your children need to move on from your previous relationship. It's important to get a bigger house so your new spouse's kids (who live on the other side of town) can come and visit on the weekends. Finding a new house will help you build a strong, loving, close relationship with your spouse and children. Given all of these reasons, you pick up the phone and call a realtor. You're ready to pursue your goal to its accomplishment.

Setting and achieving goals creates the confidence we need to keep moving along the journey of success. For each of your top three life focus areas, ask yourself the following:

1. **To experience the values you have in this life focus area, what goals must you set for yourself?** You must identify the goals that will create fulfillment in your most important life focus areas and give you more of the feelings you value. For example, let's say that in your profession, you value success. You would ask, "What goals do I need to achieve in order to feel successful in my profession?" (That's a very different question than asking, "What do I need to accomplish in my job?") Ask the same question for the life focus areas

you consider most important.

2. **What do you mean by this goal?** There are four keys to creating clear goals. First, make sure your goal is *specific*. "A better relationship with my spouse" is not very specific. "Having a weekly 'date night' with my spouse" is more defined. The clearer and more specific you are about what you want, the easier it will be to attain. Second, make sure your goal is *measurable*. How will you know when you have achieved your goal? What results do you need to see or feel? At work or with money, your goals may be very easily measured. Emotional goals, like a better relationship, are harder to quantify, but do your best to describe the desired result. Third, make your goal *realistic*. If you're making $50,000 currently, for instance, a goal of making $500,000 might not be realistic enough for you to create a plan to achieve it. You may need to set some interim goals (making $75,000 per year, for instance) that are more within your grasp. Fourth, your goal needs to be *within your control*. "Getting my child into a great college" is not under your control; "Making sure my child gets the help he or she needs to do well in school" is.

3. **What's your deadline for accomplishing this?** It's often said that a goal is a dream with a deadline. Set a realistic time frame for accomplishing this particular goal.

4. **How great will it feel to attain this goal? How will it feel if you *don't* attain it?** Self-discipline can take us only so far when it comes to putting in the work required to accomplish anything. For that extra burst of motivation, nothing beats attaching a lot of emotion to accomplishing your dreams. The more emotion you attach to getting this goal—and the more pain you attach to not achieving it—the more likely you are to persevere. When you attain this goal, how happy will you be? What difference will it make in your life and the

lives of the people you care about? How will you feel a year from now having accomplished these goals? When you combine the power of your emotions with the strength of your mind and will, you'll be unstoppable.

5. **How essential is this goal to your fulfillment?** On a scale of 1 to 10, 10 being the most important, how important is this goal to you? If you were to accomplish this goal, what level of impact will it have on your life? Life being what it is, it's very easy for some of your goals to fall by the wayside. But there are some goals that are absolutely vital for you to make progress in your life focus areas and to feel the emotions you consider valuable. Those are the goals you rate at a level 10. The goals that are 10's create a white-hot desire within you. They burn with an internal flame that is not put out by any unexpected "rain" of adversity.

6. **What priority does this goal need to have, and why?** If you have more than one goal in any area (as most of us do), you need to prioritize. List your goals in order of importance: the level 10's first, and so on. You can start with the ones that will give you the greatest sense of accomplishment, or you can make your top goal the one that will produce the greatest results. Sometimes the things we want to do the least will make the greatest difference in our lives, so prioritize your goals according to their impact. Then re-write your list of goals in order, with the most important goal first. Next to each goal, put the reason you wish to accomplish it. Your reasons must be meaningful and emotional; they need to come from your heart rather than your head.

Put the list of goals, and the life description you created in step 1, in places where you can look at them regularly—on your cell phone, computer, desk, refrigerator or bathroom mirror. Review your list frequently, so you will stay emotionally connected to the results you desire. And if you *really* want to make certain you'll achieve these goals, choose someone to whom you will be accountable. You will do far more when you make a commitment to people you care for than you will for yourself.

For goal-setting to be anything else than daydreaming, you have to put time, energy, and thought into creating goals with meaning. As my dad always told me, thinking is hard work—that's why so few people do it. However, when you spend the time to think about your life focus areas and values and create goals to achieve them, you will have enough drive to get through most obstacles and create a truly fulfilling life.

Five Key Categories of Financial Goals

Over the years I've found that anyone who handles their finances with confidence has defined goals in five basic areas. If you do not have goals in these areas, I suggest you add them to your list.

#1—EARNING: People who are financially confident set specific yet realistic goals for what they wish to earn each year, and explore ways to add more value to their business or their employers. They also may add to their earning power by starting a part-time business, or taking classes in a new skill, or increasing hours on the job if they are paid an hourly wage. (By the way, earning more also can include the efforts of other members of your family—income from your spouse and your children.) I often recommend that people set a goal to increase their earnings at least 7 percent per year. Declaring your desire and intention to earn that much can open you up to making the kinds of efforts and spotting opportunities that you may never have seen otherwise.

#2—SAVING: Most of us take the money we earn, subtract the money we spend, and whatever's left over we either fritter away or, if we're smart, invest it for our future. However, if you want to build financial confidence you must *pay yourself first*, by setting a minimum amount that you must save every month. The only way you can create financial security is to build the habit of spending less than you earn and investing the difference for your future.

Many people take advantage of automatic deductions at work that go directly into retirement accounts, and because employers often match these contributions, this is a great way to save for your future. However, as many of us discovered during the last recession, work-based retirement and pension plans are not as safe and secure as we thought. That's why I believe your first financial goal should be to save *at least* 10 to 20 percent of your after-tax income. The first place to put this money is toward establishing an emergency fund (you'll learn about that in Step 3) to cover expenses should anything affect your earning power (layoffs, termination, decrease in business income, injury, taking care of an ill child or parent, and so on). Your emergency account should be large enough to cover your expenses for at least two months, and preferably six months to a year. Even after you have created an emergency fund, however, keep putting aside that 20 percent every month. Ten percent of that will go toward covering big (usually unexpected) financial purchases/needs, like major car and/or appliance repairs or replacements, medical bills, and so on. The remaining 10 percent will go toward long-term financial goals—retirement, your children's education, and so on.

#3—SPENDING: Most of us don't think of spending as a financial goal, but without a clear spending plan (or budget), you may easily find yourself without any money at the end of the month, or falling into debt little by little. When people itemize their expenses, usually they'll tell me, "I can't believe I'm spending that much on dry cleaning (or coffee, or iTunes downloads)." Becoming conscious of your unconscious spending is a key step to greater financial success. However, the people who achieve *real* financial confidence figure out a way to spend less than 80 percent of their take-home pay each month and put the rest into savings. Make your spending goal to live on 80 percent of your take-home pay.

#4—PROTECTING: This is a category that many people forget, and yet it's arguably the most important of all. If you don't protect yourself, your family, and your possessions, you can lose everything you worked so hard to achieve in an instant. Protection takes many forms, including (1) life insurance for you and your spouse; (2) insurance on your property, especially your house, your car, and your business if you're an entrepreneur; (3) health, disability, and long-term care insurance (these will give you more financial peace of mind than almost anything else); (4) a will and a trust so your heirs will be taken care of should anything happen to you; and (5) other legal documents such as a durable power of attorney and an advanced health care directive. If you have children under the age of 18, you also need a nomination of guardian. As part of protection, make sure you include the costs of insurance in your spending plan.

#5—INVESTING: Investing means finding places to put your money where it will work for you and grow. To make the most of the money you save, you will have to invest it in things like CDs, stocks, bonds, mutual funds, real estate, businesses, and so on. For most of us, this is where we need the most objective and unbiased advice. In Step 4 we'll talk about how to find people to help you understand and choose investments that are right for you and your goals.

Go through the goal-setting process described earlier in this chapter to come up with your own specific financial goals in these five areas. Later on you'll discover some specific suggestions and strategies that will help you reach these goals.

Congratulations! You now have clarity about your personal "why"—the life focus areas, values, and goals that are truly important to you. The next step is to determine where you are today. You need to know your starting point so you can plan the pathway that will get you from where you are now to the end point of your goal. You must *collect and organize* the information that will allow you to determine your starting point, both in your finances and your life.

The Heart of the Matter

➤ The first step in building confidence is getting your life priorities straight, and discovering your personal reasons for pursuing your goals.

➤ Getting clear on your life priorities starts with having a vision that includes (1) your life focus areas, (2) the feelings and emotions you value, and (3) the goals that will help you get more of these feelings in the areas that are important to you.

➤ Life focus areas are indicators of your current priorities. To discover yours, ask, "Where am I putting my energy right now? Where *should* I be focusing my efforts to feel more fulfilled?"

➤ Values are emotions that we consider most important in our lives. We value different feelings in different areas— career versus family, for example. We also have different definitions for the feelings we value, and different ways we allow ourselves to feel these emotions. To discover your values, ask, "What feelings do I consider most important to experience regularly? How do I know when I have these feelings?"

➤ Setting powerful, compelling goals should be linked to your life focus areas and values. Your goals should be clear, achievable, measurable, realistic, within your control, and have a due date for their accomplishment. Make sure you associate great feelings to attaining your goals and negative feelings to failing to achieve them. Prioritize the goals according to the impact they will have in your life, post this list where you can see them, and find someone who will hold you accountable.

➤ There are five key categories in which you should have financial goals: (1) earning, (2) saving, (3) spending, (4) protecting, and (5) investing.

Kitchen Table Conversation

After each step of the Financial Confidence Cycle, you'll see a "kitchen table conversation," which is an example of the step in action. These are the conversations that many families have around the kitchen tables at home, discussing the challenges they're facing, and how they're dealing with life circumstances. These stories are drawn from actual conversations I've had with people all over the country. Some of the examples are composites, but all of them are based on fact.

One such clarifying conversation involved John and Susan, a married couple seeking advice on their retirement options.

John.	*Louis, we want to make sure we save enough money to retire in 20 years.*
Louis.	**That's a great goal. You did the life priorities, values, and goals clarifying exercise, right? What are the life priorities you want to focus on?**
Susan.	*Our top three are relationships, financial, and physical.*
John.	*We need to get our finances back on track after the last few years. But we've both let our health slide with all the stress we've been experiencing.*
Susan.	*And relationships with our kids and our family are always important.*
Louis.	**And with each other, right?**
John.	*Of course.*
Louis.	**What about your values?**
John.	*I value success, happiness, excitement, and love.*
Susan.	*I value love, happiness, security, and accomplishment.*
Louis.	**I'm glad to see you both have love and happiness in common. What about your goals?**

Susan.	*Besides wanting to retire in 20 years, we want to move to a one-story house at that point, and spend more time golfing and relaxing.*
John.	*We also want to be able to travel and to leave something for our kids and our grandkids.*
Louis.	**Sounds like you're planning to spend your retirement together, correct? And you have relationships as one of your life priorities? So, how's your relationship today? Do you still feel passionate about each other? Are you as close as you were when you first met?**
John.	*(reluctantly) We did go through a rough patch last year—we even talked about separating. All the financial stress wasn't easy on either of us.*
Louis.	**To really enjoy that retirement together 20 years from now, is it possible that you might want to invest some time and money in your relationship today? What if you were to set a goal of revitalizing your marriage this year? Maybe get some counseling and take a short vacation together. Get back some of the passion and connection you had when you were younger. Remember that when you retire, it'll just be the two of you. Isn't it worth investing in your relationship now so you'll enjoy spending your golden years together?**
Susan.	*He's right, John. Let's plan a long weekend away, somewhere on a beach.*
John.	*And there's a series of marital enrichment classes at church. We could give those a try. It'll be great just to spend time together today, instead of waiting until we retire!*

4

Step 2: Collect and Organize
Know Where You're Starting From

Imagine you go to speak with a travel agent to plan a family vacation. She asks you to sit down. "What can I do for you today?" she says with a smile.

"We want to take a vacation to someplace warm," you tell her.

"Lovely!" she says. "Where will you be leaving from?"

"I don't know," you reply.

She looks puzzled and asks, "How many days do you want to take?"

"I'm not sure," is your answer.

Now she's getting frustrated. "How much do you plan to spend on this trip?"

You shrug. "No clue."

She stands up and tells you, "How can I plan a vacation for you if you don't know where you're leaving from, how long you want to stay, and how much you can spend? Please come back again when you're a little clearer!"

Of course, you wouldn't go to see a travel agent not knowing where you're going and when. But every day people consult financial planners with no idea about their current financial status, or their future financial goals, or how much money they are spending and investing. To get to the goals you pictured so vividly in Step 1, you must understand exactly where you are today. You must *collect and organize* the necessary information to draw a clear picture of your current status.

(Note: While in this chapter I'll most often use the example of collecting and organizing financial information, the step applies to any goal you wish to work on.)

Unfortunately, most people who go to see financial planners do so because they are not organized, and therefore they are feeling overwhelmed and out of control. In truth, many of us organize our financial records only once a year. Can you guess what prompts us to put in the effort? Tax time. Come March or April, most of us are frantically searching through piles of papers or dozens of receipts, trying to find what we need to meet the April 15th IRS filing deadline. I know that keeping track regularly of all of the different aspects of our finances can be challenging. Income, expenses, utility bills, credit card statements, investments, insurance, loans, CDs, IRAs—we receive updates, mailings, e-mails, notices throughout the year, month after month, and filing and keeping track of all of that is a daunting task. However, *in order to build financial confidence you must start by knowing exactly where you are*: what you make, what you spend, how much you invest, and how much you have already accumulated. No matter what your goal, knowing where you are at the start will help you get to where you are going.

What's Your Starting Point?

In Step 1 you discovered the life focus areas, values, and goals that you need to work on in order to live a fulfilled, happy, successful life. You now have the end point of your journey. But to get from where you are today to that end point, you need to be very clear on exactly "where" you are today. No one can give you directions or guide you without knowing your starting point, and if you set out without a clear idea of where you're coming from, you might get to your goal by chance or luck but the odds of your getting there are very slim. On the other hand, when you know exactly where you're starting from and where you want to go, you can plan your route between those two points with relative ease.

Your plan to achieve any goal needs to take into account the size of the "gap" between your starting point and where you want to end up. You begin the process by determining where you are now in comparison to where you want to be. Here are a few examples of what I mean.

» Say your goal is to lower your blood pressure to a healthy 120/80, and your current blood pressure is 200/120 because your idea of exercise is to drive to the corner store to get another six-pack of beer. What kind of exercise program will you need to start? How often can you work out each week? What's your current diet like? Is there a family history of high blood pressure that could make things a little more difficult? Your plan to attain a healthy blood pressure is going to be different from that of someone whose blood pressure is 140/90, already works out on weekends and simply needs to increase their cardiovascular exercise to reach the goal.

» If your goal is to have a certain amount saved for retirement in 15 years, you need to know the answers to several questions to determine both your starting point and your plan to reach your goal. How much do you have set aside already? How much of your current income are you saving each year? How steady is your income? Can you plan on regular increases, or do you own a business or work for yourself and thus may experience fluctuations in your income?

» If you wish to sell your current home and buy something else, how soon would you like to buy/sell? How much do you believe you can spend on this house? Have you researched both your credit score and possible sources for a mortgage? Do you need to research neighborhoods or visit schools before you start looking for a specific home?

To attain the goals you described in Step 1, and to experience fulfillment in the life focus areas and values you believe are important to you and your family, you need a clear plan that is based not just on your vision of what you want but also on what's real at this moment. That's why your assessment of your current status must include not only a financial review but also a personal review. For each of the goals you listed in Step 1, ask yourself the following.

1. **On a scale of 1 to 10, 1 being not at all, 10 being already there, where would you rate yourself currently in this goal?** If you want to save towards retirement but only have $1,000 to put in the account today, you'd rate yourself at a 1. If you have some money saved but only enough to fund a few years of retired life, you might rate yourself a 3. If you have enough saved that you could cover basic living expenses for 10 years or more, you might give yourself a 7, and so on. (By the way, it's very normal to rate yourself at a 5 or below when you're just starting to work on a goal, so don't be too hard on yourself—the low rating probably reflects that this goal hasn't been much of a priority until now.)

2. **Describe your current status in detail.** This is the moment to be brutally honest with yourself about your current status. Think of this like an annual physical. The doctor has to weigh you, and measure your blood pressure and other vital signs to determine your current level of health. This moment of truth may not be enjoyable, but it is absolutely necessary. How can you measure your progress unless you know your starting point?

   As far as financial goals are concerned, you'll need to know the exact amounts you wish to earn/save/accumulate, and how much (if anything) you already have set aside and/or are making currently. You'll also need to know your timeline for the goal, as this will have a significant impact on your plan for its achievement. You will take different steps to save for retirement when you are 30 than when you are 55, for instance.

When you evaluate your starting-point for your goals, you may discover some surprising aspects of your current situation that need to be addressed. But without knowing both your strengths and weaknesses when it comes to pursuing your goals, you won't be able to focus your efforts where they are most needed. Again, think of it like a physical examination. If the doctor puts you on a treadmill for the first time in years and you discover that you can't run more than two minutes without becoming winded, you may not like that particular result, but it's a clear indication of an area where you need to focus if you are to be healthy and strong. In the same way, assessing where you are today as far as your goals are concerned may bring up some unpleasant or unwanted information. You may discover that you aren't as frugal as you thought you were, or perhaps your relationship isn't as strong, or your credit score isn't very high. But just like the treadmill test, unpleasant or unwanted information often is the best indication of where you need to focus your efforts. It will help you build a plan that can lead to attaining your goals more quickly, because you are putting your efforts where they are needed most.

Where Are You Today Financially?

To get to where you want to be in the future, you also have to know exactly and specifically where you are today financially. To determine this, you will need to do three things.

First, you must *collect* all of the paperwork that concerns your financial life, and get all of your financial information together. The paperwork will fall into four categories.

1. **Income information:** includes…

   » Pay records from your current employment, business, or self-employment. The record should show the totals for both your gross (your salary) and net (what you actually take home) income.

» Money you earn from sources other than an employer. If you sell items on eBay, or babysit for neighbors, or do side jobs for which you're paid in cash, you need whatever records that pertain to those activities.

» Income you receive from sources like Social Security, pensions, annuities, settlements, etc.

2. Expense information: includes…

» Household bills (utilities, food, etc.)

» Credit card bills

» Insurance (life, health, disability, auto, etc.)

» Car payments

» Mortgage payments

» Loan payments

» Taxes (federal, state, property, city, etc.)

» Education expenses for your children

» Receipts for any expenses not covered in any of the above categories

3. Investment information: includes…

» Retirement accounts

» Stocks, bonds, CDs, annuities, etc.

» Investment property

» Life insurance (with a cash value)

4. Permanent financial information: includes…

» Federal and state tax returns

» Insurance policies

» Registration and bill of sale for your cars and other vehicles (boats, etc.)

» Mortgage notes and deeds for any real estate

» Birth certificates, marriage licenses, etc.

» Stock certificates (if any), savings bonds, etc.

» Will and trust documents

(All permanent financial records should be kept in a safe, fire-proof location.)

Once you've compiled your financial information, your next step is to *organize* the paperwork you've collected. Set up file folders for each of the different categories, and put receipts, bills, etc. in the folders in chronological order. If possible, make sure you have at least a full year's worth of documentation for the different categories. If you can't manage that, collect and organize at least three to six months' worth. You will need this to create a clear picture of your current financial status.

By the way, a great way to collect and organize your information is to pick one day a month and dedicate it to your efforts. You'll be amazed at how much progress you can achieve when you put a little concentrated time into getting your finances in order. Many professionals also advocate that once you've set up your files, you simply take an hour or so on the last Sunday of the month to organize any financial information that you have received over the prior 30 days. Even though organizing your finances is something that few people enjoy doing, almost everyone I know enjoys the *result* of being organized: the feeling of being more in control of this important part of life.

Third, when you've collected and organized your information, you must *summarize* where you are. This involves using the information you've collected to determine (a) *your current expenses*, and

(b) *your net worth.* When you get ready to create your plan (which is our next step), you'll know exactly where you're starting from and how much money you will have to work with to build the financial future you want.

Summary #1: Where Does Your Money Go?

If you've ever looked at your bank balance at the end of the month and thought, "Where did my money go?" you know that nothing shakes your confidence faster than confusion as to where you're spending your hard-earned income, or worse—whether you're going to have enough to cover your expenses each month. It used to be that a lot of us were spending unconsciously, plunking down $5 a day for a fancy coffee drink or paying for club memberships that we rarely used. On My Street today, many of us are looking closely at our expenses and trying to cut costs in any way we can. But in my experience, very few of us have taken the time to calculate our monthly and yearly expenses. It's easier to say we don't know than to get clear and actually do something about our spending habits. But to build financial confidence, you *must* know these numbers—even if they're higher than you want them to be. Once you know what you're spending, you can figure out how to cut what's unimportant, pay for what's essential, and use your income to create a better financial future for you and your family.

To figure out what you are spending currently, use the worksheet on the following pages. Enter your current *monthly* and *annual* totals for the appropriate categories. The numbers you enter should include everything spent by you, your spouse, your children—everyone you consider part of your household.

My Street Money Spending Worksheet

Name: _____ Date: _____

(Please review all categories before starting.)

Category	Expense	Monthly Amount	Annual Amount
Home	Mortgage (or Rent)		
	Mortgage (Home Equity Line of Credit)		
	Extra Principal Payment		
	Property Taxes on Personal Residence		
	Homeowner's/Private Mortgage/Renter's Insurance		
	Association Dues on Principal Residence		
	Second Home Mortgage/Time Share Payments		
	Property Taxes and Insurance on Second Home		
	Furniture & Fixtures		
	Housekeeping/Cleaning & Maintenance		
	Negative on Rental Properties		
	Other:		
	Total Home Expenses	**$**	**$**
Utilities	Water		
	Electricity		
	Gas		
	Trash		
	Telephone		
	Additional Phone Lines (Internet/Fax)		
	Cell Phone Services		
	Cable Services		
	Other		
	Total Utilities	**$**	**$**
Taxes	Federal		
	State		
	City/Local		
	FICA		
	Medicare		

	Expense	Monthly Amount	Annual Amount
Taxes Cont.	State Disability		
	Other:		
	Total Taxes	$	$
Insurance	Health Insurance		
	Health Insurance Deductibles		
	Prescriptions		
	Life Insurance		
	Disability Insurance		
	Dental/Vision Insurance		
	Long-Term Care Insurance		
	Other:		
	Total Insurance	$	$
Charitable	Religious Organizations		
	Nonprofit Organizations		
	Payroll Deduction Plans		
	Other:		
	Total Charitable Contributions	$	$
Investments	Savings (Emergency Reserves)		
	Company Savings Program (FSA, HSA)		
	Retirement (IRAs, 401k, 403b, 457, Roth)		
	College Tuition Plans (ESAs, 529 Plans)		
	Other:		
	Total Investments Savings	$	$
Transportation	Car Payment (or Lease Payment)		
	Car Insurance		
	Registration Fees (DMV)		
	Gasoline/Alternative Fuels		
	Car Maintenance (Oil, Tires, Brakes, Repairs)		
	Parking		
	Public Transportation (Train, Bus, Taxi)		
	Other:		
	Total Transportation	$	$

	Expense	Monthly Amount	Annual Amount
Work Related	Continuing Ed. (Class/Conference Fees, Travel)		
	Membership Dues & Subscriptions		
	Union Dues/Professional License Fees		
	Uniforms/Tools		
	Other Unreimbursed Expenses:		
	Total Unreimbursed Work Expenses	$	$
Professional	Financial Planner		
	Accountant/Tax Preparer		
	Attorney/Legal Help		
	Therapist/Counselor		
	Other:		
	Other:		
	Total Professional Fees	$	$
Children	Child Support		
	Child Care/Babysitting		
	School Tuition		
	School Events (Support)		
	Extra Curricular/Lessons (Sports, Band, Piano)		
	Tutoring		
	Other:		
	Total Child Expenses	$	$
Food & Sundries	Food (Supermarket, Costco, etc.)		
	Specialty Food/Beverage Stores		
	Sundries (Target, Wal-Mart, CVS)		
	Breakfast —Out		
	Lunches—Out		
	Dinners—Out		
	Snacks (Starbucks, Jamba Juice, Pinkberry, etc.)		
	Other:		
	Total Food & Sundries	$	$

	Expense	Monthly Amount	Annual Amount
Clothing	Clothes—Adults		
	Clothes—Children		
	Accessories (Shoes, Purses, Jewelry, etc.)		
	Dry Cleaning/Tailor		
	Other:		
	Total Clothing	$	$
Pets	Food/Supplements		
	Treats/Toys		
	Veterinarian		
	Grooming		
	Other:		
	Total Pet Expenses	$	$
Entertainment	Parties (Birthdays, Anniversaries, Graduations)		
	Entertaining (Superbowl, BBQ's)		
	Concerts/Sporting Events/Theater/Movies		
	Books and Magazines/Music/Movie Rentals		
	Other:		
	Total Entertainment	$	$
Personal Care & Fitness	Grooming (Hair, Mani/Pedicures, Waxing)		
	Gym Membership Fees		
	Specialty Classes (Yoga, Spinning, etc.)		
	Personal Fitness Trainer		
	Sports Equipment (Running Shoes, Clothes)		
	Supplements (Vitamins, Weight-Loss Products)		
	Hobbies (Golf, Scrapbooking)		
	Other:		
	Total Personal Care & Fitness	$	$
Gifts	Birthdays		
	Christmas		
	Anniversaries and/or Other Special Occasions		
	Other:		
	Total Gifts	$	$

	Expense	Monthly Amount	Annual Amount
Technology	Electronics (TVs, Cameras, Camcorders)		
	Home Computer/Laptop		
	Cell Phones/PDAs		
	Software		
	MP3 Player (iPod) and Accessories		
	Other:		
	Total Technology	$	$
Travel	Vacations		
	Weekend Trips		
	Day Events (Theme Parks)		
	Gifts/Souvenirs		
	Other:		
	Total Travel	$	$
Personal Credit	Credit Card fees & interest—Visa		
	Credit Card fees & interest—MasterCard		
	Credit Card fees & interest—AmEx.		
	Credit Card fees & interest—Discover		
	Credit Card fees & interest—Dept. Stores		
	Credit Card fees & interest—Other		
	School Loans		
	Personal Loans (Family, Friends)		
	Retirement Loans		
	Banking Fees		
	Other:		
	Total Personal Credit Payments	$	$
Miscellaneous	Pocket Money		
	Alimony		
	Extended Family Support (Parents, Siblings)		
	Other:		
	Other:		
	Total Miscellaneous	$	$
	Total Expenses:	$	$

<u>Tips:</u>

1. The only amounts you should include for each of your credit cards are (a) any interest or fees you're charged monthly and annually, and (b) any amounts from previous years that you are still carrying over today. For example, if you took a vacation two years ago and you're still paying it off, you'd put that amount by the appropriate credit card. However, if you charged $200 on that same card for food during the month and $150 for gas, you'd list the $200 on the line where it says "Food (Supermarket, Costco)" and $150 where it says "Gasoline/Alternative Fuels." In other words, don't mistakenly list the same expense in two places—by the credit card and by what you bought.

2. When an expense is annual, divide by 12 and enter the amount in the monthly column.

3. If you don't know the amount, take an educated guess.

4. Review your check register or bank/credit card statements for expenses.

Subtracting your monthly expenses from your current income will tell you how much money you have each month to save and invest for your future.

One of the best things about collecting and organizing your information is that you see clearly where your money is going each month, and where you may have problems. Maybe you have covered your usual monthly expenses but forgot to save enough to pay for semi-annual or annual bills like insurance premiums or property taxes. Maybe you have spent more for your children's hobbies, or you've been a little too free with your credit cards around the holidays. Maybe your income is seasonal—you're a teacher who doesn't get paid in the summer, or you are a freelancer who gets paid by the job—and you're not saving enough to cover the months when your income is reduced or nonexistent. A spending worksheet is the clearest picture possible of what you spend each month to create your current lifestyle. And when you compare the annual total with your annual income, you can see whether you are in for long-term pleasure (if your income exceeds your expenses) or pain (if the opposite is true). Remember, if you make $40,000 a year and spend $5,000 less than your income, you're further along the road to financial confidence than someone who makes $1 million and spends $5,000 more than they bring in.

Summary #2: Your Net Worth Statement

The second calculation to determine where you are currently is to figure out your *net worth*. To do this, you'll figure out two numbers. First, your *assets*, which include everything you own that has value, either now or in the future. This includes your home, auto, business, other real estate, etc. (You do not deduct any mortgage or car loan amount from the value of your home or car. Those numbers go under "liabilities.") Assets include any savings, checking, retirement funds, IRAs, 401(k)s, etc. You also may have a cash value life insurance policy that can be considered an asset.

The second number you'll need is your *liabilities*, or any debts you currently owe. This would include mortgages on your home or other real estate (how much you have left to pay on them); car loans (same); credit card debt; other loans, either personal or business (including education loans); home equity loans, and so on. (Note: Liabilities are different from the monthly expenses you listed on the Spending Worksheet.)

On the following pages you'll find a form that includes the most common categories of assets and liabilities. You may need to do a little research on some of the categories, but it will be worth it, because your net worth calculation is usually a good indication of your current financial health.

Net Worth Statement: Assets

Name: _____   Date: _____

Assets	Value
Cash	$
Checking Accounts	$
Savings Accounts	$
Money Market Accounts	$
Certificates of Deposit	$
Money Market Funds	$
Mutual Funds	$
Individual Stocks	$
Stock Options	$
Bonds	$
Notes Receivable (2nd Trust Deeds)	$
Tax Deferred Annuities (Non-Qualified)	$
Individual Retirement Accounts (IRAs)	$
Roth IRAs	$
401k	$
403(b)/TSAs	$
457 Plan	$
SEP IRA	$
SIMPLE IRA	$
Profit Sharing (vested)	$
Other Retirement Accounts	$
Life Insurance Cash Value	$
Limited Partnerships	$
Personal Residence	$
2nd Residence (Vacation Home)	$
Investment Property	$
Automobiles	$
Boat/RV/Other	$
Business	$
Precious Metals (Gold, Silver)	$
Collectibles (Antiques, Jewelry, Art)	$
Other Valuable Personal Property	$
Other	$
Total Assets	$

Net Worth Statement: Liabilities

Name: _____ Date: _____

Liabilities	Balance
Personal residence mortgage	$
Home equity line of credit, 2nd mortgage, etc.	$
Auto loan #1	$
Auto loan #2	$
Credit card balance #1	$
Credit card balance #2	$
Credit card balance #3	$
Credit card balance #4	$
Credit card balance #5	$
Student loans	$
Personal loans	$
Retirement Loans	$
Other	$
Total Liabilities	$

	Total Assets:	$_____
—	**Total Liabilities:**	$_____
=	**Your Current Net Worth:**	$_____

One caution: make sure that when you figure your net worth you haven't overestimated the value of your assets and underestimated the value of your liabilities. My experience is that almost everyone overestimates the value of his or her home, jewelry, furniture, and so on. Be honest, not optimistic.

If the numbers don't look the way you would like, take heart. Knowledge is the first and most important step in taking action. Your expenses and net worth simply indicate your financial starting point. Your job is to implement the tools and lessons in this book so you can increase the amount of assets you possess and decrease the liabilities. For most of us, this starts with reducing expenses, eliminating credit card debt, and paying off any outstanding loans as quickly as possible. As you pay off your liabilities you'll see your current net worth number rise, and your financial confidence will rise along with it.

You now know exactly where you're starting from and a picture of the life you want to achieve—the life focus areas, values, and goals you set in Step 1. You are ready to close the gap by creating a plan that will lead you from Point A (where you are now) to Point B (your ideal future). And as you set out on the road to your ideal life, know that you also will be building financial confidence every step of the way.

The Heart of the Matter

➢ To attain your goals, you must be very clear exactly where you are starting from today in comparison to where you want to be. You must collect and organize the necessary information to give you a clear picture of your current status.

➢ To evaluate your starting point, rate yourself on a scale of 1 to 10, 1 being no progress toward the goal, and 10 meaning you have attained it. Once you've given yourself a rating, describe your current status in detail. Even if the assessment isn't what you want, it will give you a clear indication of the areas where you need to focus your efforts first.

➢ To assess your financial starting point, you need to collect all of the paperwork that concerns your financial life. This information falls into four categories: (1) income, (2) expenses, (3) investments, and (4) permanent financial information. Once you've collected all of this, your next step is to organize it so that you can access it easily.

➢ Finally, you need to summarize your financial information. Use the Spending Worksheet and Net Worth forms in this book. You'll also find the forms on www.louisbarajas.com.

Kitchen Table Conversation

Sam and Tanya came to see me because they want to save for their son's college education.

Tanya.   *Louis, we have one son, Mark, who's 14. We want him to go to college when it's time. We have about $24,000 saved.*

Louis.   **That's great. But there are a lot of factors other than money that will affect whether Mark gets into college and is successful while he's there. Close your eyes, both of you, and imagine Mark's future in college. What do you see?**

Tanya.   *(with her eyes closed) I see him in a cap and gown, walking to the stage and getting his diploma. He looks so happy! And I know he'll do well for himself.*

Louis.   **The key, then, is not just to have enough money so that Mark can go to college but to make sure he's prepared to graduate from college. And I've found through the years that a lot of kids go to a university and don't make it through. You want to make sure that Mark has both the grades and the self-esteem to graduate. Did you bring in all of his report cards for the last year?**

Sam.   *Here they are—we're very proud of how well he's doing.*

Louis.   **(looking at the report cards) I notice he's getting A's and B's in all of his classes except math, where he's pulling C's.**

Sam.   *Math's never been his strong suit. He's better at English and sports.*

Louis.	*Do you think that Mark's struggles with math might be affecting his self-confidence? Kids who do well in college need to have good self-confidence and self-esteem.*
Sam.	(shrugs) *I never went to college, so I wouldn't know.*
Louis.	*You're both fully on board supporting Mark's education, right? You're helping him with homework, going to all the parent-teacher conferences, setting curfews, and so on?*
Tanya.	*Absolutely—we both are.*
Louis.	*Let's look at how you can help with this challenge with math. What if you used some of the money you put aside for Mark's college fund to pay for a math tutor for him now? Or maybe a summer school math class, or test preparation for the math section of the SATs? Do you think that could help him improve his grades and maybe get a scholarship?*
Sam.	*I'll bet he'd be more confident if he could do well in his toughest subject.*
Louis.	*Sometimes the best investment we can make in our children's future is to get them the support they need today—not just academically, but with their confidence, their self-esteem, and their peer group. You both sound like great parents, and Mark's a lucky kid.*

5

Step 3: Create a Plan
To Close the Gap

Imagine you want to visit a store in an unfamiliar part of town. Do you simply get in your car and start driving? Of course not. You either (1) find the store on a map and plan your trip based on the shortest distance or most familiar route, or, more likely, you (2) look up the store on Google or Yahoo maps or MapQuest and then get a printout of directions and a map that will get you from where you are to where you want to be. And if you have a GPS on your phone or in your car, you simply plug the store's address into the device and then look and listen as the GPS gives you turn-by-turn directions as you drive. But no matter how we get directions, none of us would think of taking a trip simply by getting in the car and driving off, unless we had taken the route before or we were driving for pleasure. Yet how many of us set off on the road that we think will lead us to our goals and never plan in advance the shortest and/or best way to get there? Just as trying to reach a destination without a map is a slow and arduous means of traveling, a goal without a plan is nothing more than wishful thinking. With a detailed plan, however, you can reach your goal faster and by a more direct route. Think of the distance between your starting point and your final destination as the "gap" that your plan is designed to close.

Your plan will include a series of steps and actions that you will put into an order and sequence to lead you to your goals. It will help you make the most of the resources available to you, and prepare you in advance to handle any obstacles that may come up. This is true whether you're talking about finances, relationships, health, career—any of the life focus areas we discussed in Step 1. Your plan will be determined by three things. First, *your specific version of the goal.* Two people may have goals that seem similar, but their individual versions of what that goal looks like are very different. For example, many people share the goal of providing a safe, secure future for themselves and their families. However, "safe and secure" for one family may be $10 million in the bank, living in a $5 million mansion and having a vacation home in Hawaii, and putting their kids through Harvard without having to borrow a dime to cover the costs. "Safe and secure" for another family might be owning a small house in a modest neighborhood, buying an RV so they can travel as a family, and seeing the kids settled in good-paying jobs as teachers, police officers, or accountants. That's why it is so important to be very specific when you create your goals, and why you spent so much time writing your goals down in Step 1. (And if you haven't written your goals in detail, please go back and do it now.)

The second element that will shape your plan is the *timeline* for accomplishing the goal. Let's say your goal is for your daughter to graduate from college. Your plan for helping her to accomplish that will be very different if she's currently in first grade than it will be when she's a sophomore in high school. You'd save differently, do different things to help her keep her grades up; you may or may not be looking at possible colleges. Someone once wrote that a goal is a dream with a deadline; well, a plan to reach a goal must have a timeline so you can figure out how quickly you must make progress along the way.

The third element of your plan includes the *resources*—both inner and outer—that you can call upon as you work to achieve your goal. With a goal to lose weight, for instance, you will need to call upon inner resources of persistence, determination, honesty, and a willingness to say no to temptation as you change your diet. Outer resources may include a physician who monitors your progress, a nutritionist, a scale, the local farmers market where you can buy fresh fruits and veggies, and so on. (One of the best outer resources for attaining any goal is the loving support of family and friends. We'll talk about that in the next chapter.) As you create your plan for your goals, you'll identify resources that will help you along the way.

Your Plan to Close the Gap

There are five basic steps to creating a great plan: (1) choose your goal, (2) set your timeline, (3) brainstorm the actions you will need to take, (4) identify the resources you need to draw upon, and finally, (5) prioritize the actions that will lead you from where you are to where you want to be.

1. Look at the goals that you created back in Step 1. For each of those goals, take a sheet of paper and write one single goal at the top, with a clear description of what that goal means for you. "Getting back in shape" isn't specific enough; "Running a 10K race" is better.

2. Next to each goal, write the *deadline* for its accomplishment. I suggest that you set a deadline that is realistic yet aggressive—put a little pressure on yourself to make this goal happen. If you haven't run in years, training for a race that's a week away may be unrealistic. However, running a 10K race in two months' time is very attainable. Create a sense of urgency around the deadline for achieving your goal and you're more likely to put in the work to accomplish it.

3. On a separate piece of paper, make a list of all the *actions* that will get you to your goal. List everything that would need to happen for you to make progress. Actions to train for the race might include timing how long it takes you to run a mile today; running four times a week with a buddy; declaring

your intention to run a specific 10K race and putting some money on the line ("I'm donating $100 to the charity that's sponsoring this race"); scheduling a massage to help your sore muscles; and so on.

4. Turn the list of actions over, and on the back, draw two columns. In Column 1, list all of the *inner* resources you will need. These may include discipline, persistence, pride, and so on. It's very important when working on your goals to recognize exactly the kind of emotional and mental strength you're going to need to get you through any obstacles or tough spots. In Column 2, write all of the outer resources you can draw upon to help you attain your goal. For example, to accomplish the actions listed in #3, you'd need a stopwatch/timer, a running buddy, good running shoes, a masseur, and so on.

5. In this step you will finalize your plan by prioritizing your actions. On the sheet of paper with the goal at the top, write the actions in the *order* you believe they need to occur for you to reach your goal—for example, getting a good pair of running shoes might need to happen before your first run. Then put a star next to the *most important* actions on the list, based on your situation. Finding a running buddy might have the biggest effect on your progress; for someone else, a weekly massage might be the most important support. By taking care of a few key actions immediately, you can get a jump-start on your goal.

   As you prioritize your list of actions, inevitably other actions will pop into your mind as being necessary or helpful. Maybe you should load up your iPod with music for your runs, or plan different routes so you'll keep from being bored. Ask yourself, "What haven't I thought of that might help me make progress?" Add anything that comes into your mind to your list, and put it in its proper place in the order of tasks.

Finally, next to each action write the date by which you want to accomplish it. This will help you track your progress and keep moving forward on your goal.

Once you have your plan, rewrite it so that it's clear and concise, and then keep it handy. This is your guideline for the actions you will be taking between now and the due date you set for yourself. Check your plan at least once a week, mark the actions you've completed, and make notes of your progress on other actions. If you are falling behind, do your best to get back on track rather than resetting your deadline. Revise your plan as necessary, but do your best to keep on track with your original goal. In Step 5 we'll talk about systematic paths to success to keep you moving forward on your plan.

Creating Plans for Your Financial Goals

To attain the kind of success that most of us living on My Street want, you must have clear financial goals and the plans to achieve them. By building a plan for your financial goals you can anticipate setbacks, build in back-up strategies, and most important, be clear on the small steps and timelines you will need to close the gap between where you are and the financial security and confidence you desire.

If you look at most of your goals, I'll bet there is a financial or money component involved in many of them. If you want to lose weight, you can certainly do it by walking barefoot on city streets and eating less of what you already ingest; however, you may find it much easier to reach that goal if you can spend some money on resources like a personal trainer, a gym membership, quality fresh food, and supplements. If your goal is to create a better relationship with your spouse, your plan may include spending more time with him or her. However, that goal could include a couples' weekend retreat, or a vacation, or hiring a babysitter so you can have a night away from the kids—and all of that takes money.

In the same way, the plans for your financial goals need to take other aspects of your life into account. Say your goal is to save enough so you can retire at age 65, travel, and never have to work again. Sure, you can figure out how many years you have to save and invest, how much you'll need to make on the money you set aside, how much your lifestyle will cost—all of those are logical elements of a retirement savings plan. But are you planning to travel with your spouse? Should you plan on investing some time and money today in keeping your relationship strong? What about your health? If you don't take care of your health today, will you enjoy that retirement or will you be sitting somewhere with an oxygen tank and a nurse at your side? Nothing in life happens in a vacuum; everything in your life is connected. That's why you must create comprehensive plans for both your life goals *and* your financial goals.

On the flip side, we don't have financial goals simply to have a particular number of dollars; we have financial goals so we can have and do certain good things in our lives. Here are some financial goals that many people share. Notice that none of these goals has a particular dollar figure attached to it. Every goal is about doing something *with* money, not about acquiring money for money's sake.

Common financial goals include....

» Saving for retirement so you can live a better quality of life in your golden years

» Buying a home or a second/vacation home to spend more time with your family

» Preparing to get married or have children to experience more love in your life

» Saving for your children's education to give them a good foundation for their future

» Starting a business to build financial independence

» Creating an emergency fund to cover unexpected financial challenges

» Buying investment property to create income for the future

» Purchasing a large item such as a boat, motorcycle, etc., to have more fun

» Celebrating a life event (a wedding, anniversary, graduation, etc.) to create wonderful memories

» Taking a vacation to relax and/or experience new adventures

When I speak with people about creating a plan for their financial goals, I often use the metaphor of building a house. You have a clear idea of what you want your house to look like—your goal—but in order to turn that vision into an actual residence, you need a detailed plan or blueprint: something that shows you exactly where the walls will be, where the plumbing and electrical wires will be located, how each of the appliances will fit into the kitchen, and so on. You also need to know your timeline and your action plan, so that your house goes up efficiently and is well built. Third, you need to know what resources you require—a contractor, subcontractors, suppliers, and so on. And finally, you need to make sure your foundation is solid so you can build the house of your dreams.

One of the great things about creating a financial plan is that you begin to see if there are any weaknesses in your financial foundation that need to be shored up before you begin to build. Based on all of this, and having completed the Spending Worksheet and Net Worth Statement in Step 2, you should have a very clear idea of your foundation—your starting point. If necessary, any financial plan may need to include improving your current foundation. For many people, building a better future starts by strengthening the foundation of their current financial "house" as represented by the Spending Worksheet and Net Worth Statement. Are expenses too high based on their current income? And are most of those expenses optional, meaning that there's a lot of money going toward unnecessary credit card purchases, vacations, and large phone or cable bills and not enough money being put towards savings? Or perhaps money needs to be invested in ways that will help people achieve other goals, like finding a better job, which would require getting some further training, or helping a child go to college by sending them to summer school so he or she will improve their grades.

Creating plans for your financial goals uses the same process I described earlier. In order to create a secure financial life for yourself and your family, you need to know where you want to be (the goals you created in Step 1), where you are today (you did that in Step 2), and how you will get there (your plan). You build the plan for your financial goals in the same way you did your life goals. The elements of your plans are going to be very specifically tied to (1) your current situation, (2) your goal, (3) your timeline, and (4) the resources you have access to in pursuing your goals. You can refer back to that part of this chapter and create plans for the financial goals you have set for yourself.

The Five Key Elements of a My Street Money Plan

Remember in chapter 1 we spoke of the importance of mindset, money, and meaning? A My Street Money plan identifies your mindset, establishes the values and goals that mean the most to you, and then organizes your money to help express your full potential to live your best life. While your individual financial situation will direct your specific plans, you also must consider the five important elements of building a solid financial foundation for you and your family. You learned about these five areas in Step 1; below you'll find some further recommendations for actions to take. If you make progress in the following areas, you will walk down My Street with confidence, knowing that you have taken care of you and your family.

#1—EARNING

» Create a budget of what you want your lifestyle to look like and, based upon that number, figure out backwards what income you'll need to live a financially confident life. For example, if you want to own a $400,000 house, take a vacation every year, buy a car every five years, put your three kids through college, and retire on an income of $75,000 per year, run the numbers and see how much it would take to pay for the mortgage, all of your family's living expenses, the vacation, the car, and so on. Then calculate the cost of the kids' education, and how much you'd need to have saved to produce an income of $75,000 per year in retirement.

» If your desired numbers look daunting, take heart—and come up with a plan to increase your earning by at least 7 percent this year and for the next 10 years. (You may be surprised at how quickly you can afford the lifestyle of your dreams.) Base your plan on adding more value to your employer and/ or having your business add value to more customers. If you want some ideas on how to add more value, please see my book, *Overworked, Overwhelmed, and Underpaid.*

» Protect yourself professionally. Continually sharpen your job skills, network with family and friends, or start searching the Internet for potential employment opportunities. If you own your own business, keep educating yourself on recent developments in your field, what your competition is doing, and how you can increase your value to your customers while managing your costs carefully.

#2—SAVING

» Create a "confidence fund": a cash (emergency) reserve at your bank or credit union (accounts are now insured by the FDIC for $250,000 per depositor). The rule of thumb is to save enough to cover two to six months of living expenses at a minimum. Some people prefer to have 9 to 12 months of emergency reserves, depending on the industry in which they work.

» Save at least 10 percent of after-tax income each month. Make a commitment to pay yourself first by setting this money aside each month to save and invest. (This is in addition to any contributions you already make through work—I hope you are making the maximum allowable contribution and taking advantage of every single dollar your employer matches.) If possible, set up a program that automatically deducts 10 percent from your monthly income and puts it into a savings or investment account.

#3—SPENDING

» Consciously and purposefully review your spending, and look for places you can reduce expenses and put more money into savings. Your ultimate goal is to live on 80 percent or less of your after-tax take home pay. See if you can reduce your spending by 5 to 10 percent a month until you reach that goal.

» Try to identify at least five places where you can reduce expenses and put the money towards savings. My friend David Bach calls this the "latte factor"—the money we spend almost unconsciously that could be used instead to help us build more secure financial futures. For example, if you spend $4 each workday on one coffee drink, that adds up to $20 per week, or $1,000 a year (assuming 50 weeks of work per year). That $1,000 could be used towards a nice family trip—or, more important, could be invested in your children's education or your retirement.

» Are there areas where you need to *increase* your spending as an investment for your future? Are you allocating enough money to care for your car, your home, yourself? Are you investing anything in skills training for your profession, or for your children to help them do well in school? Make sure your spending plan takes such expenses into account.

#4—PROTECTING

» Make sure that you have health insurance for you and your family. If your employer doesn't provide health insurance, look for plans that have high deductibles to lower your monthly premiums. One health problem or accident can wipe you out financially, so at the minimum you must get a major medical insurance policy.

» Make sure you and your property are insured, and review your policies (homeowner's, auto, life, disability, long-term care, etc.) annually. You may need to change the amounts and kinds of insurance you have based on your current and future circumstances. A good insurance agent will work with you to match your needs to the appropriate policies.

» Review your estate plan and other legal documents. Make sure your wishes are known and your estate can pass to your family easily when you and/or your spouse are gone. Name your family trust, or someone whom you can rely on, as the beneficiary on your accounts (savings, life insurance, etc.) held for your minor children. I also suggest you put written instructions for your wishes in your will about things like cremation versus burial, or the distribution of family jewelry or heirlooms.

#5—INVESTING

» Contribute at least 10 percent of your income (if not the maximum) to your retirement plan at work. If your employer matches your contribution, consider that as extra, not part of your 10 percent. Make sure to diversify your investments in your retirement plan. (We'll speak about diversification in chapter 10.)

» Establish additional investment accounts, such as IRAs and education accounts for your children. Again, diversification in these accounts is key to long-term growth and protection of your money.

» Hire a fee-only Registered Investment Adviser to review your investments. You'll learn more about such advisers and how to find the best one for your needs in Step 4.

Remember when you are creating your plans for these five areas to frequently ask the question, "What *haven't* I thought of when it comes to this particular financial goal?" Recently I was speaking with a gentleman who had set up a plan for building his restaurant so he could pass it along to his sons. In reviewing what he had created, however, I noticed that he didn't have health insurance. "It's just too expensive," he protested. "We need to buy new equipment for the restaurant this year."

"Building a bigger and better restaurant won't do your sons much good if you get sick and bankrupt the business before they're ready to take over," I told him. "In all honesty, you're constantly complaining about health issues; your plan for a secure financial future for your family had better include taking care of your health and buying health insurance to make sure you're covered in case of a serious illness."

The final plan that I suggest that everyone have in place is a *contingency plan*. While many of us share the goal of creating a safe, secure future for ourselves and our family, we rarely think that included in that goal should be planning for the unthinkable—accidents, trauma, long-term illness, loss of property, and so on—and the inevitable—death. No one likes to think about worst-case scenarios, but you owe it to yourself and your family to plan for difficult times. That's why you need to have the protection of insurance and an estate plan in place. That's why you must have an emergency savings account to cover monthly expenses should you not be able to work. That's why you have an emergency plan in place for earthquakes, floods, tornados, and other natural disasters, so your family will know what to do in those terrifying moments. When you take a little time to ask, "How can I prepare for the worst?" and develop plans to handle those situations, you'll sleep much better at night, with far more confidence, knowing that your family will be as safe and secure as you could make them.

The best thing about developing clear plans with timelines is that you'll see how much difference you can make in your financial confidence with relatively small changes in each of the five areas: earning, saving, spending, protecting, and investing. Think about it: a 5 percent difference in each area adds up to a 25 percent increase in your financial wellbeing. A 10 percent difference in each area equals *50 percent* more financial security and confidence for you and your family. Remember the old joke about how you eat an elephant—one bite at a time!

If you want to construct a plan on your own, there are a wide range of great books that will give you a lot of strategies to get you to your financial goals. But while you can build a plan to reach your financial goals by yourself, there's a lot to be said for talking with someone about the best steps to take given your specific situation. When it comes to creating a truly comprehensive financial plan to build your confidence as well as your net worth, I suggest that you consult a fee-only Certified Financial Planner™ who can make specific recommendations based on your situation. In chapter 6 we'll talk about choosing the right financial support team to help you create and carry out your My Street Money plan.

Once your plans are in place, you must communicate and collaborate, to gain the support of the people around you and ask them to collaborate with you as you embark upon the road to financial confidence. That's the focus of Step 4.

The Heart of the Matter

➢ To create a plan to achieve any goal, you must know your specific version of the goal, your timeline for its accomplishment, and the inner and outer resources you can call upon along the way.

➢ Five basic steps to create a great plan are: (1) identify the goal, (2) set your timeline, (3) brainstorm the actions you need to take, (4) identify the resources you will need, and (5) prioritize your actions to get you to your goal.

➢ Once you have your written plan, check your progress at least once a week. Revise your plan as needed, but try to keep to your original deadline.

➢ Your My Street Money plan should include all five categories of financial confidence: earning, saving, spending, protecting, and investing.

Kitchen Table Conversation

Cathy, a single mother, wants to set up a plan to care for her two young children in case anything happens to her.

Cathy. *Louis, I make a good income and I've already saved a lot. But I recently got divorced and my husband isn't in the picture anymore. I need to make sure my kids are taken care of in case I die.*

Louis. **Okay, there are three aspects to consider when creating an estate plan. First is the legal side— you need a will, a trust, a durable power of attorney, and so on. Second is the financial side, and third is the personal side. What do you have in place so far?**

Cathy. *I have a $500,000 term life insurance policy in my name. And I'm seeing an attorney next week to set up a trust to ensure my estate goes to the kids and not to my ex-husband. I'm so glad you told me about putting my assets in a trust so my kids can avoid probate and get access to the money right away.*

Louis. **You told me your children are minors—exactly how old are they?**

Cathy. *Tommy's seven, and Melissa's four-and-a-half.*

Louis. **Have you chosen a guardian for them?**

Cathy. *My sister and I once said that we'd take care of each other's kids if anything happened to us.*

Louis. **I know these kinds of conversations are difficult, but better to have them now than for something to happen to you and your kids have nowhere to go. You should have a nomination of guardian**

	form that gives your sister legal guardianship of your kids in the case of your death.
Cathy.	*And I can still name my sister as trustee, right?*
Louis.	*Yes—then she'll be their legal guardian and manage the trust for the benefit of your children until they come of age. Now let's look at the financial side. You said you had a $500,000 term life insurance policy. Why that amount?*
Cathy.	*That's what my husband had, and I just went to our insurance agent and told him to give me the same thing.*
Louis.	*Life insurance isn't just something we have just so our heirs will get a sum of money when we die; it should be designed so that the death benefits from the policy will give your kids the lifestyle you would want for them. And with young children, you need to think about replacing income not just today but also the income you'd be earning 10 to 15 years from now, as well as paying for their college tuition and expenses. I'd suggest that you make your term life insurance policy big enough to replace your income until your children reach age 24 rather than 18. Today kids are staying at home longer, so you should build in some cushion.*
Cathy.	*I'll talk to my agent and ask him to give me some options.*
Louis.	*Speaking of insurance, who is the beneficiary of your current life insurance policy?*
Cathy.	*My kids.*
Louis.	*Cathy, an insurance company isn't going to hand a check for $500,000 over to minor children.*

> *They won't get the money until they're 18—and even then you don't want to hand that kind of money over to teenagers. You should name your trust as the beneficiary. That way your trustee will manage the insurance money for your children until they're adults.*

Cathy. *I'll make sure to name my trust as the policy's beneficiary.*

Louis. *The last aspect of estate planning is sometimes the most difficult, and that's the personal side. You need to talk with your sister and other family members to let them know your wishes. I also suggest you look at getting a durable power of attorney and an advanced health care directive, or living will, in case you're hurt or ill and can't speak for yourself. You also need to make sure your paperwork is organized and in a location where your heirs— or in your case, your sister—knows where everything is. And lastly, you need to have a talk with your kids.*

Cathy. *But they're so little!*

Louis. *They should know that if anything happens to you that they're going to live with their aunt and she'll take care of them. You don't need to scare them, but one of the best gifts you can give to your children is the certainty that they'll be taken care of no matter what.*

Cathy. *That's what I want. Thank you for the clarity.*

6

Step 4: **C**ommunicate and **C**ollaborate
Create Buy-In and Build Your Team

Imagine that you're at work one beautiful summer day, and you get an inspiration. You call your spouse and say, "Honey, instead of eating dinner at home tonight, let's pack a picnic, take the kids and go to the park!" You don't even notice that your spouse isn't enthusiastic about the idea. At 5:00 p.m. you hop in your car and race home. You can just see it: you and your spouse sitting on the grass, drinking iced tea or lemonade, while your kids run through the park, the sounds of their happy voices drifting toward you as the sun sets in a blaze of red and gold.

Well, the evening isn't *exactly* what you envisioned. You walk into the kitchen to see your significant other (looking less than thrilled) putting stuff in the cooler and saying, "I wish you had called earlier; I have some work I need to catch up on tonight. And we need to stop at KFC to get some fried chicken as I didn't have time to fix anything but a green salad and drinks." No problem—you keep your spirits up as you go into the family room. "Who's ready to go to the park?" you ask happily. Your teenage daughter is lying on the floor, ear glued to the phone, talking with one BFF and IM-ing a second BFF on her laptop. Your ten-year-old son sits on the sofa, playing yet another video game (you've lost track of which one is his latest favorite). When you put a hand on his shoulder, he shakes you off. "Not now—you'll mess up my score!" he says. You stand in front of them and say, "Look, you two, we're going to the park for dinner, and that's it! And no cell phones, no laptop, no video games, no DVD players, nothing. Get ready—we leave in five minutes." You stomp upstairs, the sounds of their groans and protests fading away. Your perfect family evening is a disaster before you even put one foot out the door. Why? You failed to get your family on board with your idea first, before you took any other action to turn your idea into a reality. You didn't create *buy-in*, the support we all need when we want to put our plans into action.

Even the best-laid and best-intended plans can fail when everyone affected doesn't agree with either the outcome or the plan. If people feel their needs and wishes haven't been taken into account, there will be limited buy-in at best, and active discouragement or sabotage at worst. For example, have you ever worked at a company where the boss announces a blanket policy that affects all employees without ever asking for the employees' input or comments? Often that's a recipe for questioning, disagreement, foot-dragging, and other indications that the employees don't want to go along with the decree. In the workplace, sometimes you have to deal with that kind of behavior; however, when it comes to creating your goals, you want—and need—as much support as you can get. Therefore, if you're smart, you'll work to create buy-in for your goals from the people you care about.

Creating buy-in always begins with *clear communication*. You must communicate your goals with your team, and collaborate with them to implement the plan you created in Step 3. However, the first person you must communicate and create buy-in with is yourself. If you don't believe you can accomplish your goals, or you aren't ready to do what it takes to create the results, you won't succeed. Let's say you want to get in shape. You go to the gym and sign up for a session with a personal trainer who gives you a detailed plan for reaching your goal. "If you do these exercises five times a week for the next six weeks, you'll be in great shape!" she tells you. However, you think,

I'm not sure I can take that much time away from everything else I have to do. So you go to the gym three times in the first week; the following week you go only twice; and the next week you drop the whole thing. Getting in shape just wasn't important enough to you. You didn't have enough emotional buy-in to pursue the goal.

Take a look at the goals you set in Step 1, and the plans you created for them in Step 3. Are you ready to do what it takes to follow your plans? To persevere, you must be emotionally invested—that's why you wrote down all your *reasons* for wanting these goals as part of Step 1. Take a few moments to read your reasons for achieving your goals, and make sure they create strong enough emotions in you to make you follow through.

Sometimes creating buy-in requires looking at your goals from a different perspective. Take the goal of getting in shape. If your only reason for this goal is to look good at the pool this summer, that might not be enough motivation to get you to the gym five times a week. However, if your daughter were getting married in six months and you wanted to look your best and make her proud on her special day, you'd probably be at the gym as often as it took to reach your goal. Look at your reasons for wanting your goal and see if there might be other reasons or people that could motivate you more.

Here's another example of the power of a new perspective to help increase buy-in. Once a couple in their mid-fifties came to talk to me about creating a financial plan for their retirement. In looking over their Spending Worksheet, I noticed there was nothing entered in the category of health insurance. I asked them about it, and they replied, "We don't have health insurance—it costs $700 a month for the two of us. We're both healthy, and we'd rather put the money into a retirement account."

However, health insurance is a vital part of any sensible financial plan, so I encouraged them to take a different perspective. "Look at this not as insuring your health but as protecting your finances," I told them. "You told me you want to retire about 10 years from now. If you chose to put that $700 a month into a retirement account, yes—you would have about $84,000 saved in 10 years. But do you know how much it costs if either of you have an accident, or need to have an operation in the next 10 years? A lot more than $84,000. And if either of you should be diagnosed with a chronic health problem like heart disease or cancer or diabetes, without health insurance you could end up having to spend *all* of the money you've saved for retirement and even have to sell your house—and possibly have to file for bankruptcy, too. Purchasing health insurance for the both of you is actually the best investment you can make in your long-term financial security." The couple had never thought of health insurance in those terms, but after our meeting they added it to their monthly expenses.

Just like a weak foundation won't support a strong building, weak reasons won't support strong goals. To create greater buy-in, you may have to change the way you look at your goal to build the strong foundation you need to achieve it.

Creating Buy-In with Others

Once you have buy-in with yourself, it's time to create it with your support team—your spouse or significant other, family members, business associates, and so on. We all have people around us who will be affected by the goals we pursue, and reaching your goals will be easier if you take the time up front to enroll your family, friends, and colleagues in supporting your efforts. Conversely, if you think you can pursue goals without consulting your family, you're in for a rough ride. Whenever a married man or woman would come to my office alone and ask to create a financial plan for their family, I would say politely, "Please bring your spouse the next time." I knew from long experience that a financial plan created by only one member of a couple would inevitably produce disagreements and lack of support from the other.

I believe there are three keys to communicating your goals clearly to others. First, *be honest* about what you are trying to do and the support you would like to receive. Sometimes we soft-pedal our requests because we don't want to offend people, or we're afraid they may say no. However, it's far better to be honest up front about the support you need, so you can come up with ways to minimize any not-so-positive effects. For instance, say that your goal is to go back to college and finish your degree, and you find a program that requires you to take classes three nights a week. However, your family is used to you coming directly home from work every night, and pursuing your goal will mean less time spent with your family. It may mean your spouse has to prepare dinner alone more often, and you may not be able to help your kids with their homework every night. The best thing is to make an honest request for their support and then create a plan that takes both your needs and theirs into account. Can you take time together on the weekends to make meals to freeze and then eat during the week? Can you make it a point to check your children's homework and tuck them in on the nights you're not in class? Can you get your kids and spouse to help you with your studies, so they feel they're part of your goal? No matter how you accommodate their needs, being honest about what you need from your team up front will make getting their agreement easier.

The second key to creating buy-in is to *be realistic in your expectations* of yourself, other people, and circumstances. As someone once told me, unrealistic effort is attainable but not sustainable; and the goal of realistic expectations is to produce sustainable results. It's better to ask your spouse to agree to put aside $50 a month for a child's education starting when that child is born, for example, than to scramble to put together a large sum of money when that child is in high school. Set realistic expectations—control what you can, and don't worry about what you can't—and you're much more likely to keep making the steady effort that will lead to your goals.

The third key to creating buy-in is for you and your support team to *be patient*. Achieving a goal is like climbing a mountain; at the beginning it can seem that you're making very little progress because the base of the mountain is so big. Many people become discouraged and quit halfway up the mountain because they don't feel they're moving fast enough. They didn't think it would take so long to save for a car, or to get the degree, or to start the business. So they simply stop trying and all their effort is wasted. However, if they're patient and simply keep going, they will reach their target. The more time and effort you put in, the closer your goal will be. And if you keep persevering, you will succeed.

Most of the time it can be easy to get support from the people who care about you, simply by telling them your goal and the reasons you want it, and then asking for their help. However, it is possible to run into two specific problems. First, your "support" team doesn't really believe in your ability to reach your goals; and second, they're afraid that your success might have a negative effect on your relationship. Here are some tips to handle such a dilemma. I'm going to use the example of getting support from your spouse/significant other, but this will work with other family members, core business associates, and so on.

> » Show your written goal to your partner so he or she is clear on what you wish to achieve. Clearly articulate your ideal outcome. What will your goal look and feel like when you reach it? Make sure that your description includes the positive impact of this goal on your partner and your family. State your goal as a completed vision. For example: "When I'm healthy and fit I'll have more energy to do things with you and the kids. And I'll be around to see our daughter graduate and get married."

> » Show your partner the plan you created in Step 3 that will lead to your goal and ask for their ideas, suggestions, and support. If they start to tell you why you'll never achieve it, gently request that they not tear down your ideas or efforts. Offer them support in reaching their own goals.

> » Describe again how great it will be for your relationship and the family when you attain this goal. Resolve to take the first step together to accomplishing your dreams. And take the first step quickly; show your partner that you're serious about pursuing this goal.

Communicating About Finances

Nowhere is creating buy-in more important than when it comes to finances and relationships. Marriage and money can be a touchy subject. In fact, the number one excuse for divorce in America is said to be financial stress. I say "excuse" because I don't think that the cause is financial stress; I believe that communication breakdown is the real problem. When I talk with couples about finances, I often find myself playing the role of mediator. Even if they say they have shared goals—like saving for their first home—their approaches often seem completely opposite. One wants to save conservatively, the other wants to risk everything for bigger returns. One partner thinks they have to scrimp and save every penny for the future, the other wants to put some aside while still having a nice lifestyle today. The result? Anger, upset, the silent treatment, shouting matches; couples feel that they just don't understand each other anymore. But when I cut to the chase, we discover that they simply have two very different ways of approaching the same goal.

Different environments, family histories, and cultures shape how each person views the world. These differences cause us to be liberals or conservatives, spenders or savers, and so on. And while we may agree about the issues we face, we rarely agree on the best approach to solve them. It's the same with joint finances. I'm sure that you've known couples where one partner makes all the money and takes on responsibility for all financial decisions. That may be fine—unless the other partner feels powerless without access to his or her own funds, or perhaps feels as if they have no input into this very important part of their life together. On the other hand, there are couples where both partners make money and they keep their earnings completely separate, each paying for their own expenses and splitting any joint costs of the household. That may be fine, too—but some people in these kinds of arrangements say that their relationship feels more like roommates than a marriage. And keeping money separate doesn't mean there will be fewer arguments about the "big" areas of financial responsibility, like raising children, saving for retirement, or large purchases like an automobile. Difficulties can arise around finances even in the best-matched couples, creating resentments, tensions, and arguments that can pull them apart. That's why I believe that the best and smartest thing that any couple can do is to communicate clearly, early, and often, about finances. Major financial decisions need to be made jointly, and ideally should be a result of discussion, collaboration, and compromise. But all of this starts by making sure both partners agree first, on their joint financial goals, and second, on the plan(s) to achieve them.

Earlier I gave you some ways to ask for support from a spouse/significant other/partner. Here are a few additional tips to help you communicate and collaborate with your partner about finances.

Tip #1: *Establish your financial ground rules as a couple early on.* Many couples tell me that talking about finances was one of the toughest conversations they had before marriage—harder than talking about sex. Yet dysfunctional finances have broken up more marriages than problems in the bedroom. Sit down with your partner and get clear about how you each feel about finances and money. This money discussion should include things like…

> » Who makes it

> » Who spends it

> » Who controls it

> » Who pays for what

> » Who's responsible for bills, taxes, and so on

> » Whether to have one joint bank account or a joint account for household expenses and separate personal accounts

> » How to make decisions about big purchases

> » How much to save monthly and yearly

> » What kind of investments you are comfortable with

> » How much is okay to risk when it comes to investments

» What kind of an emergency fund is needed

» How much insurance you should have, and what types

» Your short- and long-term financial goals as a couple

Be prepared to repeat these discussions whenever your circumstances change (the birth of a child, an inheritance, a new job, and so on) or whenever you are faced with financial decisions that affect both partners. The key principle is, *never assume* you know what your partner will say or feel about finances. It's better to ask and confirm you're right than to assume and be wrong.

Tip #2: *Make sure both partners educate themselves about their finances.* It used to be that whenever a couple would come to see me for financial planning, one partner would bring in all the paperwork and the other would sit there without saying anything. When I would ask the silent partner their opinion about the couple's finances, he or she would say, "My spouse handles that—I don't know anything about money." Luckily, that scenario happens far less frequently these days, but it's still true that often one partner takes charge of the couple's finances while the other doesn't really know the details. However, I believe that both people in a couple need to educate themselves about money, so they can make mutual decisions about their financial goals. If one partner wants to handle the day-to-day bookkeeping, fine; but the other partner should know where the money is going and how it is kept and invested. After all, the financially savvy partner may not always be around. After a divorce or the death of a spouse, people can feel overwhelmed because they never made it a priority to learn and understand enough about their finances. Communication and collaboration means making sure both partners know enough about finances so they can make intelligent decisions, now and in the future.

Tip #3: *Never set a financial goal for your family without consulting with your partner first.* You may have personal financial goals, like earning a certain amount of income, getting a certain job, saving for retirement, and so on. However, if any of these goals affect your family, you should consult your spouse. Setting aside a certain amount of your take-home pay, for instance, will be much easier if you discuss it with your spouse before you start bringing home a smaller paycheck. If your partner understands the reasons and can see the benefit of such a decision—and better still, if you involve your partner in deciding how much to set aside, for example—then he or she is more likely to support your efforts. When it comes to goals, collaboration can produce faster results and a stronger relationship.

Tip #4: *Put your finances into the context of the bigger goals of your relationship.* Hanging on the wall in my office I have a stock market chart showing the ups and downs of the market over the long term. Funny thing about the stock market, though—the overall trend has always been up. Sure, there are obvious down cycles (like the Great Depression, the inflationary 1970s, the dot.com bubble, 9/11, and the recent "Great Recession"), but in the long run, they look like momentary pauses when you compare the dips to the upward trend of the overall chart. It's amazing how many times I have used that stock market chart to talk with couples about their marriages instead of their investments. When there are conflicts in a relationship—about finances or anything else—it's all too easy to get caught up in the problem and forget all the other areas of the relationship that are still good. Even if a momentary disagreement seems very serious, in the big picture of your relationship it's probably nothing more than a momentary dip. To get through the problem, you must focus on why you got married in the first place and why you are together as a couple. Visualize what your relationship will be like once you weather this problem and others that are common in all marriages. Above all, believe in each other and in the upward trend of your relationship.

Tip #5: *If there are conflicts, check your life focus areas and values for clues to resolve them.* Do you know your partner's core life focus areas and values? Life focus areas and values subconsciously drive our behavior, so if you and your partner disagree on finances, it's very possible that the conflict lies not in what you want, but in how you believe you should get there, which is based on what you believe is most important. I recently met with a couple, both of whom described their top five values as spirituality, marriage, children, friends, and career. When I met with each partner individually, however, the husband listed his values one way, while the wife's list was different. Here are the two lists, side by side.

Husband:	Wife:
1. Career	1. Children
2. Friends	2. Marriage
3. Marriage	3. Spirituality
4. Children	4. Friends
5. Spirituality	5. Career

Do you see any possible conflicts due to the different priorities husband and wife placed on the same values? I always ask couples to discover their life focus areas and values before we talk about anything financial. I've found that it's extremely important to discuss openly any potential values conflict and identify possible harmonious resolutions before they start setting goals and creating plans as a couple.

If you go through the values process with your partner and discover potential conflicts, talk them through and see if you can come to some kind of compromise. For instance, if your partner puts career first, he may want to invest all your spare funds in a new business venture. However, if you have children at the top of your list, you may want to save your family's money to put your children through college or throw them a big wedding. Both of these are valuable and worthy uses of a couple's money; therefore, you are going to have to talk it over together and see what you can work out. Maybe you can start the business first, and then dedicate a portion of the profits to your children's education. These kinds of discussions may not be easy, but they are always worth it. You may even discover that working through these kinds of thorny issues will make you stronger as a couple, because each partner feels their needs have been heard, respected, and valued.

Collaborate: Find People to Help You Achieve Your Goals

In Step 3 you should have created a list of outer resources you would need to reach your goal. Look at your list and notice how many of these resources are people rather than objects or services. People are always the most important factor in anyone's success; they are your core team, collaborating with you to provide personal and professional support for your goals.

Forming your team takes three steps. First, you must *identify who you will want and need as part of your circle of support*. You already should have developed a version of this list in Step 3 (identify outer resources), but take a few moments to review your list and see if you need to add other people. If your goal is to go back to college, for instance, you might need a tutor, or perhaps a study partner—but what about a babysitter to stay with your kids while you're in class? (If your goal is financial, you will need very specific professionals as members of your support team. I'll cover that later in this chapter.) Make sure your family is always included as part of your team—if they are on your side, achieving any goal will be much easier!

Second, *find the best people for those roles*. Some team members, like your family, are already in place, but you will need to locate, select, and enroll other people to help you. Say you have a goal of getting a promotion at work. Your family has agreed to support you in taking extra training and working longer hours. You also may be able to enlist the help of your boss and/or co-workers in letting you take on a high-profile project. You might ask your supervisor, or someone at the HR department, what training would serve you in being promoted. If you enroll in a class, you could speak with the professor or trainer about your goals and see if they can help you. In all of these cases, you must (1) make your goal and your desires known, and (2) enlist the assistance of others in reaching your goals.

Third, *ask your team to collaborate with each other*. I recently heard about the value of collaboration between team members from a couple who had consulted an estate planning attorney to set up a trust. The attorney told them, "I'm concerned that your current life insurance isn't adequate. You bought a $250,000 policy when you first got married, but now you have two children—and that $250,000 won't be enough for the surviving spouse and children to maintain your current lifestyle. Can you give me the name and number of your insurance agent?" And right then and there, the attorney called the agent, and within a short time the couple had a new policy. That's the kind of communication and collaboration you want to see among the people who are supporting you.

There are two things to remember when it comes to collaboration. First, the best time to create and nurture these collaborative relationships is *before* you need them. Build relationships with many different people; they will enrich your life whether or not you're pursuing a goal with them. This leads to the second thing you must remember: collaboration is a two-way street. It's much easier to ask people for help when you've been helpful to them. You'd be amazed how often the people you meet through church, professional organizations, volunteer activities, or simply those you are nice to in line or around town can end up being your realtor, or helping you find the best loan, or lead you to a great school for your child. Your kindness, your willingness to collaborate, and your efforts on others' behalf will come back to benefit you tenfold.

Your Financial Support Team

Part of building financial confidence is to enlist a team of professionals who can help you create and follow through with a plan that will achieve your financial and life goals. However, not all financial professionals are created equal: there are good ones and shoddy ones, so you need to understand what to look for in your financial advisers. But always remember: *you* are hiring *them*. Even if you think they know more than you about finances, it's still your money they will be dealing with. Therefore, you have to be comfortable with them, and also make sure they will do a good job for you.

Here are some rules for hiring any type of financial professional.

Rule #1: *Choose someone who works with finances for a living.* Just because Uncle Harry made a killing in the stock market doesn't make him the best adviser for your investments, and just because your best friend did her trust on the Internet doesn't make her the appropriate person to draw up your estate plan. When it comes to your finances, you want someone who has the competence, credentials, and character. Look for professionals who can provide you with the best advice, not amateurs who may not have all the information to create a plan suited to your needs and goals.

Also, make sure your advisers focus on one specific area or discipline. If you choose a financial adviser who is trying to juggle five different specialties or has their main focus on something other than finances, I have found that often you get less than great advice across the board. When someone is great at what they do, they don't need to earn income from multiple sources. Don't go with jack-of-all-trades who sells investments, insurance, prepares taxes, and so on, or someone who does finances as a sideline. Hire financial advisers that are specialists in their own fields.

However, even if you have family in the financial services field, I believe that you should never hire a family member. If you think family arguments over money are bad, try the arguments that break out when a family member gives you "professional" financial advice that doesn't work out! If you have a family member in the finance business, ask for a referral.

Rule #2: *Choose people whose primary job is to advise you, not simply sell you something.* Any good financial adviser is going to need to be paid somehow—and with financial professionals as with everything else, you get what you pay for. The person who sets up an IRA for you at a bank may be able to sell you mutual funds or tell you about stocks "free of charge," but they make their money from commissions on your trades (whether or not your stocks or mutual funds go up in value). Ask any financial professional you consult how they will be paid. Is he or she going to charge you a commission, a flat fee, an hourly fee? You also need to know up front how much these services will cost you. Don't fall for the "It's not going to cost you anything, my company is going to pay me" trap. You always pay, one way or another, so it's better to know what the cost will be right at the start. Most professionals worth their salt will charge for their advice rather than offer it "free with purchase."

Rule #3: *Hire based on competency, not price.* When you entrust someone with your money, you want quality and competency, not the best deal. Most of the time, you'll find the higher fees are more than offset by better results—and greater peace of mind for you. How can you find competent advisers? Good financial professionals will have credentials in their particular fields. Someone who has a credential in their industry has made the effort to study for and pass rigorous exams in their area of expertise. There are credentials for financial planning, tax preparation, insurance, and so on. Most advisers will list their credentials on their business cards or in any written material about their business. This doesn't assure you that they're any good, but it does promise you that they care about meeting the minimum standards for their industry and maintaining certain continuing education requirements.

I also recommend you look for advisers with experience. Statistics show that 80 percent of people in the financial services industry leave the profession within five years. You don't want to be the guinea pig of someone who is just starting out—your money is too important to allow someone to make his or her mistakes with it. When hiring a financial adviser, look for someone with (1) at least 10 years' experience, (2) professional credentials, (3) a great reputation, and (4) a proven track record of success in their field. (I suggest you research advisers with the professional associations in your area. You'll find a list of professional associations on my website, www.louisbarajas.com.) Choose trusted advisers with impeccable reputations in their profession and community. Ask for referrals from people you trust and admire. Interview all financial professionals and ask questions. Always ask for references, and check them. Make sure you feel comfortable with this person; some professionals do not want to take the time to manage smaller accounts, or to explain their recommendations to people who are new at investing. No matter how much you have to invest or how new you are to finances, you should feel that your advisers appreciate your business and will take great care of you.

Rule #4: *Make sure your advisers customize their recommendations to your particular situation.* Imagine going to see a personal trainer who never asks you your fitness goals or if you have any physical problems. Instead, he hands you a boilerplate exercise plan and says, "Just follow this and you'll be fine." You'd probably walk out, right? But you see this same attitude in some financial professionals; they simply try to fit you into one of their boilerplate plans, insurance products, mortgages, and so on. That's not the kind of person you want on your team. Instead, look for advisers who are willing to put in the time to get to know you, your goals, your financial circumstances, your history, and your individual needs. Look for an adviser who (1) asks questions about your short-term and long-term goals, and takes into consideration what is important to you, (2) reviews your current comprehensive financial situation, and (3) prepares a plan specifically for you that aligns your financial goals with your life goals.

I also believe that great financial professionals regard educating their clients about money as equal in importance to getting them high returns. Look for advisers who encourage you to ask questions at every stage of the process and who are willing to explain things in language an average person can understand.

Rule #5: *Review your finances and investments regularly.* Your financial advisers can't do all the work. You have to do your part, by providing accurate information, by asking questions until you are satisfied that you understand the answers, and above all, by working with them to create and then follow a plan that makes sense for your financial goals. Remember, however, no one cares about your money the way you do, and therefore you are ultimately responsible for taking care of it. You are the captain of your financial team. Therefore, if you see anything in your statements or plans that you don't understand, ask about it. Paying attention to your finances will save you a great deal of pain and loss in the long run.

Some Possible Members of Your Financial Team

Who you need on your financial support team will depend on your particular situation and stage of life. Below you'll find a few broad categories of professionals, an idea of the services they offer, and what to look for when it's time to choose one to suit your needs.

Financial Planner: looks at all of your finances and puts together a plan that will help you meet your goals, including retirement, education for your children, etc.

What to look for: Choose a financial planner who

» Is a Certified Financial Planner™ *and* a Registered Investment Adviser. Only a registered investment adviser can look at your overall financial situation and give you investment advice.

» Asks questions about your short-term and long-term goals, and takes into consideration what is important to you.

» Reviews *all* your investments, financial statements, and insurance policies, including employee benefits, before recommending any type of solution.

» Prepares a financial plan tailored to your needs and specific situation.

» Tells you how he or she is getting paid—either by charging a fee or receiving a percentage for investing and/or managing your account.

Insurance Agent: specializes in advice about different kinds of insurance policies—life, disability, health, property and casualty, and so on.

What to look for: Find an agent who

» Is a Chartered Life Underwriter®. This is the highest designation of expertise in the insurance industry.

» Can advise you about and sell competitive insurance products with different types of insurance companies. You want someone who will help you find the best policy for you, not the best policy his or her company offers.

» Reviews *all* your insurance needs, including health, life, disability, auto, homeowner's, renter's, long-term care, and umbrella.

» Focuses on your needs, not theirs. Some policies pay very high commissions up front, and unethical agents may try to steer you toward these policies. If you feel this is the case, find another agent who will put your needs first.

» Doesn't see insurance as a solution to all your problems. A good agent will be aware of the benefits of different kinds of financial solutions and encourage you to do what's best for you and your family.

Tax Preparer: Since tax codes change almost every year and penalties for incorrect tax returns are very high, most of us would benefit from having professionals prepare our taxes.

What to look for: Find a tax preparer who

» Is a full-time, licensed tax preparer, Enrolled Agent (EA), or CPA. If you have been audited in the past or think you will be audited, stick to an EA or CPA who can go to the audit for you. If there are legal issues, find a Tax Attorney.

» Has a reputation for preparing returns correctly, not for getting big tax refunds. Remember, you're responsible for the accuracy of everything you submit on the tax return; claiming ignorance in an audit doesn't work. Always make sure the tax preparer signs the return, and then you review it before submitting it.

Estate Planning Attorney: has been trained to help you set up an estate plan to be sure your assets go where you want when you are gone. Also helps you minimize the legal and tax consequences of passing your estate to your heirs.

What to look for: Hire an estate planning attorney who

» Is an estate planning specialist.

» Reviews your current assets and financial plans and makes recommendations based on your desires and needs. Not everyone needs a trust, for example, but most of us need a will, an advanced health care directive, and, if you have minor children, a nomination of guardian form.

If you want more specific information on any of these categories of advisers, please visit www.louisbarajas.com.

Remember, your financial advisers are a reflection of who you are and what you want. All good financial professionals want their clients to understand their recommendations and strategies, and are happy to answer questions and educate their clients. Before you put a dime of your money with anyone, make sure you are comfortable with the financial adviser's professionalism and integrity. And then be prepared to work actively with your team to build the financial future you desire. Your financial advisers can only suggest, guide, and provide you with options; you're the one who must do the work of saving, investing, and following the plans. And ultimately, you and your team will reap the rewards of your joint efforts.

Luckily, there are ways to make your efforts easier. In Step 5 you'll learn how to set up paths to success that can double the effectiveness of your efforts and allow you to reach your goals more quickly. And you'll understand the importance of checking your progress consistently as you work toward building your financial confidence.

The Heart of the Matter

➤ One of the first actions in your plan to attain your goals must be to create buy-in—support from your family, friends, and colleagues.

➤ Creating buy-in begins with clear communication, starting with yourself. Make sure you have strong reasons for achieving these goals.

➤ There are three keys to communicating your goals: be honest, be realistic in your expectations, and be patient.

➤ To get support from your spouse/significant other, family, or business associates, do the following: (1) show them your goals and tell them how they will benefit; (2) show them your plan and ask for their support, and offer them support as they pursue their own goals; (3) take the initial steps toward the goal together.

➤ Lack of financial buy-in can create problems in relationships. To communicate with a partner on finances, do the following: Establish financial ground rules early; make sure both partners educate themselves about their finances; never set a financial goal without consulting your partner; view your finances in the context of your overall relationship; if there are conflicts, check your life focus areas and values to help resolve them.

➤ Assemble a team of people to help you attain your goals. To form a team, you must identify the roles you need people to fill; find the best individuals for those roles; and ask the members of your team to collaborate with each other.

➢ Make it a priority to assemble a great financial support team by following a few simple rules: choose someone who works with finances for a living; choose people who will advise you, not try to sell you something; hire based on competency, not price; make sure your advisers customize their recommendations to your situation; and review your finances and investment regularly.

➢ Possible members of your financial team include a financial planner, an insurance agent, a tax preparer, and an estate planning attorney.

Kitchen Table Conversation

Heather and Tony had brought their financial records for me to review and make recommendations. A week later they returned to go over the results.

Louis.	*I have a few simple changes and recommendations that will create a more secure retirement for both of you.*
Tony.	(looks over plan) *These look okay.... But what about the house?*
Heather.	*We're upside down on our mortgage. We can't even start to look at retirement until we deal with that.*
Louis.	**Let me check the numbers from your Net Worth Statement. According to this, you currently owe around $420,000 on the mortgage, right?**
Heather.	*But we paid $450,000, and our home is only worth $400,000 now!*
Louis.	**You're upside down by $20,000. Is that what concerns you?**
Tony.	*It's not just the amount. Our neighbors had to sell their house at a big loss. We're afraid that if we wait any longer to sell, our house value will keep going down and we'll end up taking a bigger hit. I know we said we wanted to look at our whole financial situation, but this has to take precedence.*
Louis.	**Okay, then, let's address it. Do you like your home?**
Heather.	*We love it. When we moved in, we said it was our dream house.*
Louis.	**Do you like the neighborhood?**
Tony.	*Other than the fact that the property values have dropped, yes.*

Louis.	***And are your kids happy there too?***
Heather.	*They love it. They have so many friends in the area, and they love their school.*
Louis.	***If you weren't worried about losing money, how much longer do you see yourselves living in this house?***
Tony.	*At least until the kids are grown: another 15 to 20 years.*
Louis.	***Are you concerned about your family business? Any problems paying your mortgage every month?***
Tony.	*We took a hit when the economy was in trouble, but now things are back on track. We're keeping up with our payments just fine.*
Louis.	***So, you love your home, you love the neighborhood and the schools, and your kids are happy there. You can afford your monthly mortgage payment, and I see from your paperwork that you still have an emergency fund to cover contingencies. The earliest you'd want to move is 15 to 20 years from now. Do you think that your house might recover its value by then, should you want to sell?***
Tony.	*Probably.*
Louis.	***I know that on paper it might look as if selling is the smart move, but you have to take other factors into account than just money. Based on the quality of life you have in your home, your current financial situation, and the fact that you won't need to sell for many years unless things change radically, what's the best decision for your family?***

Heather.	*(She sighs, relieved.) When you put it like that, keeping the house makes sense.*
Louis.	**We can set up a plan that will ensure that you can keep your home and still have a secure financial life for you and your children.**
Tony.	*(happy) Thanks—we really didn't want to have to sell our home.*

7

Step 5: Commit and Compare
Find Proven Paths to Success,
Automate Your Actions,
and Check Your Progress Consistently

Have you ever made New Year's resolutions and even created detailed plans for accomplishing them, only to find yourself the next December 31st looking at your list of resolutions and wondering why you never actually did anything to make them happen? Many people never take the first step toward their goals, and as a result, all their resolutions and plans remain merely words on a piece of paper. To make any kind of progress, you have to take the first step, and the next, and the step after that. You must *commit* to taking the steps that will turn your goals into reality.

"Knowledge is power" is a common saying, but I firmly believe that knowledge is only *potential* power. You can have all the knowledge in the world, but if you never apply it, it won't have any impact in your life. The first key to successful commitment is *action*. Thinking determines what you want, but action determines what you get. Here's an example. Several years ago I consulted with a family who owned a restaurant in Los Angeles. The business had been in the family for two generations, and the father wanted to pass the restaurant on to his sons, who were both in their twenties at the time.

We came up with a very safe, detailed plan for growing the business and training the sons to take over. Recently I happened to pass by the restaurant and decided to stop in. I was amazed to see the father still behind the counter, greeting customers and taking them to their tables. The older son was at the cash register, glumly ringing up guests' tickets.

"I thought you'd be retired by now," I said to the father. "What happened?"

He shrugged. "Business has been bad sometimes, good at others…." He hurried away to walk a couple to their table. As soon as he was out of earshot, the older son said to me, "Business has been just fine. My brother and I have been after him for the last five years to let us take over the way you outlined, but he won't do it. He's been too afraid to put the plan into action. My younger brother got tired of waiting, so he moved to San Diego and opened his own restaurant, and I'm thinking about joining him. I can't keep on working here as a cashier while my dad works himself to death." Because the father hadn't taken action on his plan, the business had lost one son, and it looked like it would lose the other. This thriving restaurant, which had been in one family for generations, ran the risk of being closed or sold to someone else, simply because the father didn't have the courage to follow through on his plan.

Taking the first step on your plan can feel like an enormous effort and a lot of risk. However, a plan on paper is nothing more than a pretty picture of your possible life, until you take *action* to make it real. This is where faith comes in. To get to the point you want to reach—with your spouse, your family, your business, or your life—you have to do things you've never done, and take risks you've never taken before. You are going to be uncomfortable; that's the hardest part of commitment. As part of your action plan you'll seek and receive the education, knowledge, and help you need, but you still will have to walk out in faith and say, "This is what I want to do." Will it work out every single time? Of course not. But if you don't take action, you're *guaranteed* that your plan won't come to pass. You have to have faith and take the first step. I also believe that even if your first step is small, you must take action *immediately* on any goal that you set. Implement at least the first step of your action plan in the first 48 hours after you set a goal, and make a commitment to devote at least 15 minutes a day to taking further action towards its accomplishment. Even 15 minutes a day can start to turn your goal into a reality.

The second key to commitment is *consistent follow-through*. If you've ever gone to the gym in January, you've seen the people who have decided to get in shape after the first of the year. But how many of them are still going to the gym in February, putting in the consistent effort that will truly get them in shape? You need to create a habit of taking consistent action as you pursue your goal. Small, consistent actions can create far greater results than a single, big, splashy effort. Have you heard of the term "compound interest"? The power of compound interest is based upon small efforts made consistently through time. We talked about the effect of compounding in chapter 2—how someone who starts saving $2 a day at age 20, invests the money and averages an 8 percent rate of return year over year would have almost $330,000 saved by age 65. However, someone who waited until age 45 to start saving would have accumulated only about $40,000 by age 65. Always remember that because of compounding, the best time to start taking even small actions is always *right now*. Big, small, or in between, consistent action is the only thing that will get you to your goals.

The Most Direct Road to Your Goals

Not too long ago a friend of mine was going from San Diego to Long Beach, California. Her GPS was on the blink, so before she left home she downloaded directions from Google maps. Now, she had driven from San Diego to Long Beach before, but it had been a while, and she trusted Google to give her the most direct, easiest route.

Big mistake. As many of us discover when we rely on maps from the Internet, or even on GPS, sometimes the directions we get don't show the easiest way to get where we are going. My friend spent a good 20 minutes driving through surface streets in Long Beach, fighting traffic, avoiding street closures, and making a couple of illegal U-turns to reach her destination. Later she found out that she could have taken two freeways that would have put her exactly where she wanted to go. It might have been a little further mileage-wise, but it would have saved her a lot of time and aggravation.

Reaching our goals is pretty much the same thing as finding the best driving route from point A to B. While there are many different ways of accomplishing any goal, some are easy and others more difficult and time-consuming. But just like the freeways that my friend could have taken to reach her destination sooner, certain methods of accomplishing goals—like getting a new job, or saving for a long-term goal, for example—have already been laid out by other people through the years. These are proven *paths to success* for attaining these goals. One of the best ways to accelerate your progress toward your goals is to compare your plan to a proven path to success.

I define a path to success simply as a specific, tested way for getting from point A (where you are now) to point B (where you want to go—your goal). If your goal is to buy a house, for example, a path to success might include saving for a down payment, checking your credit score, applying for a mortgage, finding a neighborhood you'd like to buy a house in, choosing a realtor, and so on. All these tasks will be part of your path to successfully owning a house.

Your path to success for any goal will depend upon three factors: first, where you want to go (that is, the goals you chose in Step 1); second, where you're starting from (which you discovered in Step 2); and third, how long you plan to take. For instance, if you want to learn conversational Spanish because you're planning a vacation in Argentina to celebrate your wedding anniversary, you might choose a different path than if you suddenly have to take a business trip to Spain next week. And if you took a little Spanish when you were in high school or college, your path to success for brushing up your skills may be different than if you have to learn the language from scratch.

You need to make sure that you have the right paths to success that will help you reach your goals as quickly and efficiently as possible. How do you create your own personalized paths to success? You begin by writing down all the detailed tasks you will need to do in order to achieve your goals. These detailed tasks are the specific steps for the action plan you created in step 3. Your path to success will tell you the *best* ways to take those actions that will produce the desired result. Let's take the goal of getting a raise at work. Your plan might include researching salary standards for your company and industry, drawing up a list of your latest accomplishments, talking with your boss about a raise, and so on. That's a great series of *actions* you could take to get your raise. However, for each action you'll need a path to success to create the best result. If your action is the "what" you want to accomplish, the path to success is the "how" to reach it the best possible way. What's your path to success for researching your industry to find out what others like you are paid? Will you search the Internet, go to the company's HR department, call a friend who's in the same profession, consult professional organizations, and so on? What's your path to success for talking with your boss and requesting a raise? Your path could include going in prepared with your list of accomplishments and the value you'll be able to add in the next year; rehearsing and role-playing your interview before the appointment and having your spouse or co-worker act as your boss; and finally, a back-up plan should your request be refused.

One of the most valuable sources of simple, effective paths to success is a *role model*. Find others who already have attained your goal so you can adopt their paths to success. In the above example, do you know someone in your department who requested and received a raise? Can you speak with him or her and find out how they did it? Even if you don't copy what they did exactly, often there will be elements that you can adapt to help you succeed as well.

The key to choosing a role model is to find someone who has already done what you want to accomplish, not just someone who says they know the way. If you want to improve your relationship with your kids, find a role model who has a great relationship with his or her children. If you want to start a small business, find someone who has already established a successful enterprise. If you want advice on investing, look at the adviser's track record and make sure he or she has done a good job whether the market's up or down. Success leaves clues, so try finding them before you start your journey. If you don't know anyone personally who has attained your goal, then read about someone who has. You'll find both inspiration and practical paths to success in the examples of great role models.

Automate Your Actions to Achieve Success Faster

If paths to success are our road maps, *automating the actions* we take on those paths will make it easier to stay committed. For example, you don't have to think about making time for your spouse when you have a "date night" scheduled weekly. You don't have to worry much about selecting exactly the right investments if you consult a good investment adviser and create a plan for building a diversified retirement account, and invest a specific amount each month according to your plan. Automated actions help make our paths to success easier and more practical. Very few people can rely on self-discipline to attain their goals; they need to automate their actions to keep making progress in good or bad times.

Look at the plans you created in step 3. To discover the paths to success for those plans and how to automate your actions, ask yourself the following questions.

1. **With the steps you wish to take to accomplish this goal, what's the best path to *success* to adopt?** For example, suppose your goal is to save a certain amount of money each month for the next three years to put toward starting a new business. You could take the following actions: (a) earn more money, (b) cut expenses, or (c) a combination of the two. Each action would require a different path to success. What would be the best path to success for earning more? Could you work longer hours? Take a second job? Start a small version of the busi-

ness you ultimately want to have? There are dozens of paths to success you could follow to earn more money. In the same way, there are dozens of paths to success for cutting expenses. Take a look at your actions and see how many different paths to success you could take to accomplish that part of your goal. Be as specific as possible about the steps you need to take.

2. **Is there a *role model* you can follow, someone who already has gotten the results you wish to create?** Role models can be people you know, examples you discover in books, in the media, and so on. Look at the role model's story and ask, "What did he or she do to get these results? What can I do based on their example? What path to success did they take that I can adopt to help me reach my goals?"

3. **For each of these paths to success, what *automatic actions* can you set in place that will make it easier to achieve your goals?** Make sure your automated actions are very practical. To save money, for example, many people automatically deduct a certain amount from their paychecks and deposit the money into a separate savings or interest-bearing account. Because the money "disappears" before they have a chance to spend it, it's easier to build savings consistently. Automating your actions may take a little work at first, but once in place, it should be relatively effortless.

The reason to follow proven paths to success and to automate your actions is clear: simplicity is usually your greatest friend when it comes to accomplishing your goals. Your paths to success should be easy, practical, and automatic; that's how you know they will truly lead you to the results you desire.

Check Your Progress Regularly to Stay on Track

The best way to build the muscle of consistency is to monitor your progress regularly and *compare* your progress with your action plan and your timeline for reaching your goals. Monitoring your progress frequently is critical, because if you wait too long you might end up way off track, with valuable time and energy lost. You need to keep checking your efforts on a regular basis, to make sure you are on track. What's the best way to monitor your progress? Establish in advance specific *benchmarks* to evaluate if you are on the right course. Think of it like the steps of building a house. The contractor has to build the foundation by a certain date so he can put in the flooring, then set up the frame for the walls, then install the wiring, then put up drywall, and so on. A good builder knows these benchmarks, sets the dates for their accomplishment in advance, and then checks the job's progress at regular intervals.

I believe it's also important to set a schedule for checking your progress toward the benchmarks you set. How often you check your progress will depend on your goal. If you want to build a house, for instance, you don't need to check the contractor's efforts every hour; the amount of progress would be too small to track efficiently, and you may find yourself getting frustrated and losing interest. However, if you checked the building site only once a month, or once every three months, you might not get the chance either to celebrate your wins (the drywall is up!) or to get things back on track if you're not making the kind of progress you want. Set up a schedule for checking your results that will keep you motivated and enable you to evaluate your results efficiently and effectively.

To help you set benchmarks and evaluate your progress, answer the following questions for each goal.

1. **What specific benchmarks do you need to set to help you make regular progress toward this goal?** Financial benchmarks could include (a) a specific amount of money set aside, (b) a specific percentage of income saved, or (c) specific actions taken. Decide what benchmarks you need to set that will help you evaluate your progress toward this particular goal.

2. **When will you assess your progress? How frequently will you check in?** This will depend on the benchmarks you have chosen. If your benchmarks have to do with specific actions, set a reasonable amount of time to accomplish what you have said you will do. However, I recommend that the amount of time is no longer than a month to three months. If you check in less than four times a year on a goal, you run the risk of getting way off course by the time you get around to noticing.

The journey to your goals isn't something that's accomplished in a week, month, or year, so you can't measure every day and expect to see big results. When you were young, did you ever measure your height to see how much you'd grown? Maybe you were so eager that you asked your parents to measure you every day (maybe every hour) to see if you'd grown any taller since the last time. If you measured that often, would you notice a difference? Probably not. But if you waited a month or three months, you'd almost certainly notice some kind of change. Growth toward your goals is often a gradual process. But if you measure on a regular basis, you'll see just how much growth is possible in what seems like a relatively short time.

What to Do If You Get Off Track

When you monitor your progress, you're assessing how well what you are doing is working. You do this by asking yourself two fundamental questions: first, "Where am I now?" and second, "Where is this in relation to my ideal goal or outcome?" If you're not making the kind of progress you thought you would be, you need to make some adjustments. Face it: even the best-laid plans are going to need to be revised. Life happens. People get laid off. The market takes a downturn. A new baby arrives. The kids need braces. Your vacation gets canceled or postponed. You fall off the diet wagon and put back on 15 of the 25 pounds you've lost. We all get off track at times, so it's important, first, to acknowledge the setback, and second, to resume our efforts as quickly as possible. You want to catch the problem when it's still small and get back on track immediately. Ask yourself the following questions.

1. **Where are you now? Is this where you said you would be in your progress toward this goal?** This is not the time for excuses or reasons. Just make the clearest, most honest evaluation of where you are in relation to where you said you would be.

2. **What do you need to do more/differently/less in order to achieve the progress you want?** If you've missed your target, don't beat yourself up. Instead, you must evaluate what you're doing, figure out what's not working, and change your approach.

If by any chance you find that you are off track in your journey to your goals, there are several remedies. First, go back and review your paths to success and automated actions; it could be that there are better ways to reach your goals. Second, have someone help you determine if what you are doing is on target; if your goal is financial, get a second opinion from a professional guide who makes their living helping people to reach their goals. They'll have ideas for paths to success that you might never have considered.

If you change your paths to success and automated actions and yet you're still not getting the results you want, it may be due to motivation. Go back and review your major life focus areas and values to see if the goal you have chosen is truly as important to you now as when you first made it a priority. *If the "why" is not big enough, then you will never find the "how" to achieve your goal.* Your reasons won't be compelling enough to create the energy that will be needed to reach the end of your journey.

I believe that if you're following the steps in this process and taking consistent action, you'll find monitoring your progress is a joyous step. You'll get to see how well what you're doing is working. You can also make corrections early, when it's easy to do so. And you'll get a chance to connect emotionally with the value of your progress, both in your life and the lives of your family. In truth, the best way to monitor your progress on your journey to your goals is with *internal* benchmarks. When you measure your efforts regularly, you'll find yourself experiencing certain feelings. These internal "guideposts" include peace of mind, calmness, happiness, reduced stress, a sense of progress and a brighter future, deeper relationships, and more balance and integrity. Pretty wonderful rewards for your efforts— and the more you monitor, the easier it is for you to experience these feelings regularly.

10 Key Financial Paths to Success

When it comes to traveling the road to financial confidence, there are certain "routes" that almost everyone should use. These "routes" are the 10 *key financial paths to success*. Each path to success has a series of automated actions to make your progress easier and faster, and benchmarks you can use to make sure you stay committed and on track to your goals. These ideas are simple, practical, time-tested, and proven to work. Some of these steps you can do alone, others will be easier if you hire a guide (a financial professional) or buy a map (a book on tax planning or a software program, for example). I suggest you review each path to success and implement at least a portion of it as part of your plan for building financial confidence.

Path to Success #1: Get Organized

You should have gotten your current financial documents organized as part of Step 2. However, keeping your financial documents straight takes ongoing effort, so make it part of your weekly schedule. *Automated actions*: (1) Set a time each week to organize your finances. Don't allow anyone to interrupt you; make it mandatory. Then review your investments, bills, expenses, income, etc., once a month, in the context of your financial goals. (2) Purchase an organizer to put all your important financial information in one place. (3) If you need clarity on your financial documents, schedule an appointment to meet with a professional financial adviser. *Check your progress*: Monthly on your financial records organization. Schedule yearly appointments with your tax adviser and insurance agent to review your needs. Check your credit reports and credit score yearly.

Always do a comprehensive financial review and update your plan at year's end.

Path to Success #2: Track Your Expenses

You need to track where and what you are spending your money on, and make a goal to cut your monthly expenses by at least 5 to 10 percent. Most of us will never miss one dinner out or premium cable channel—but that money, invested over time, can make a major difference. Creating and sticking to a spending plan ensures that you put your money where it truly matters. Part of controlling your expenses is to pay down your consumer debt as quickly as you can. While I'm a big believer in saving and investing, most of us are paying more in credit card interest than we could earn on our savings. Set up and follow a debt repayment plan, and as your debts get smaller, increase the money that goes into savings and investment. And avoid new credit card debt! *Automated actions*: Record your expenses weekly. You can use a financial program like Quicken, or a ledger or a notebook. You also can use the Spending Plan Worksheet in Step 2 (you can download a copy at www.louisbarajas.com). An expense report or budget will show you where to cut expenses and help you reallocate money from things that don't matter to things that do. *When you should check your progress*: At a minimum, check your expenses monthly. If you need to adjust your spending to save more, do so immediately. Remember, it's the little, daily "dings" to your bottom line that can drain your bank account without your knowing it. Eliminate the little expenses and you'll have more money for the things that really matter.

Path to Success #3: Build a Cash Reserve for Confidence

Lack of financial liquidity (that is, available cash) creates undue stress and can keep you in a job or home or situation that you hate. Conversely, knowing you have cash on hand to cover your basic expenses can give you a greater sense of security than almost anything else. *Automated actions*: The best way to build a cash reserve is to pay yourself first every paycheck. Set aside at least 10 percent of your income each month before you put money toward expenses. While this may sound difficult, when you see the "emergency cash" account growing each month, you'll experience more peace of mind. Put this money in a savings account, money market account, money market fund, or short-term bank certificate of deposit (CD). Your goal is to save enough cash to cover a minimum of two months' worth of expenses. (I usually recommend a minimum of six months, but for most people two months is a great place to start.) This money is not to be touched except in an emergency like losing a job, unexpected medical expenses, and so on. Put any bonus, tax refund, gift, or unexpected winnings straight into your cash reserve. You won't miss the money, and it will help you sleep better at night knowing that you are covered in case of financial difficulty. *When you should check your progress*: Monthly. If you're not meeting your savings goal, adjust your plan and strategy immediately.

Path to Success #4: Have a Written Plan for Your Goals

Take the time to plan your future; it will give you more certainty and help you deal with challenges more effectively. You need a clear picture of where you want to end up, financially and professionally, in order to make the greatest progress. *Automated actions*: At least once every year, create, write down, and/or review your financial goals and your plan to achieve them. If you're off track, revise your plan to get as close to your goals as possible. *When you should check your progress*: For yearly financial plans, schedule a review in December or January. In addition, at tax time, anytime you meet with a financial professional, or your situation changes in any way, you should update your long-term financial plans.

Path to Success #5: Protect Yourself from Unexpected Events

We don't like to think about things like being in an accident, or having our homes burn down, or losing a spouse. Yet if we don't prepare, those kinds of major catastrophes can destroy us (and our families) unnecessarily. Make sure you protect you and your family from any worst-case scenario. Review your insurance policies— health, life, disability, auto, homeowner's (or renter's), and long-term care—to make sure that you are covered for the major catastrophes of life. *Automated actions*: Schedule an appointment to review all your policies with an insurance professional, and ask him or her to coordinate your policies to make sure you are buying the best insurance at the most affordable price. Notice I said "affordable," not "cheapest." Often cheap insurance comes with a very high price—in terms of poor coverage, lousy service, and unfulfilled promises. Focus on quality insurance companies to make sure your insurers will be there when and if you need them. *When you should check your progress*: I suggest that people review their policies at least a month before any changes are scheduled to take effect. Examine your policies to see if you need to change your coverage or providers. For example, many health insurance plans will tie rate increases to your birthday. Auto or homeowner's insurance must be renewed by certain dates. Make sure to review the policies early enough so that you can research alternate companies or coverage levels.

Path to Success #6: Do Occupation Planning

Are you currently earning what you're worth? Sometimes we get too complacent about our jobs, and we don't make the career moves that might be to our advantage. Or we stay where we are out of fear that we won't be able to find another position. Very few people ever review their earning potential when preparing a financial plan. Check to see if you truly are doing what you love and are getting paid according to the value you provide. *Automated actions*: Research your occupation so you know what others are earning for the same job. If you're being paid less than the average wage for your field, put together a proposal for a raise. If you are turned down, evaluate the reasons given and, if you feel they are valid (for example, you've only been doing the job for a short while), make your case in a couple of months. If you feel the reasons aren't valid, you may wish to start looking for another job with a different company. I believe everyone should have a system in place so they can apply for another job at a moment's notice. Keep your resume up to date, and think about sending it out every now and then to test the job market. You can also see a professional career consultant to discuss other employment opportunities. Part of your occupation planning should be to take full advantage of your job benefits package. If your employer matches your contributions to the company 401(k), take advantage of that money. If you get tuition reimbursement at work or you can create a Health Savings Account (HSA) to cover unreimbursed medical expenses, do so. Become knowledgeable about what's offered through your work and take advantage of anything that's applicable. *When you should check your progress*: Most businesses have open enrollment periods for health insurance and/or retirement plan contributions. Use these times to evaluate your occupation planning. Review your status at least once a year, as well as anytime your job situation changes.

Path to Success #7: Save Taxes through Planning, not Preparation

Most people will pay more in taxes in their lifetime than they will ever pay for their home. Therefore, the goal of this path to success is to minimize your tax liability. (One way to know that you are not doing enough tax planning is if you either get a large refund or owe money each year.) You must evaluate what you are currently paying in taxes and ensure you are keeping as much money as is legally possible. *Automated actions*: You might want to have your taxes prepared by a qualified professional. Look for one who does taxes for a living, and who can make recommendations for reducing your taxes by maximizing your deductions. If you don't want to use a professional preparer, I suggest you buy one of the good tax preparation software packages that will walk you through every legal deduction. And once you've lowered your taxes to the point where you feel you have done all you can, take the additional money and invest it instead of spending it. That way, you're gaining a double benefit from your efforts. *When you should check your progress*: Tax preparation is not tax planning. Tax planning—figuring out how to reduce your taxes as much as legally possible—should be something you do throughout the year, not in the weeks before you file your return. I suggest that in the month after you file your income taxes, evaluate your situation to see if you can make any changes that will help you save on your taxes for the current calendar year. And make sure you have all your tax documents ready by mid-February so you aren't giving them to your tax preparer at the last minute. On average, a tax professional prepares around 100 returns the week before April 15th. Your return will definitely get much greater attention if you give your documents to the preparer as early as you can.

Path to Success #8: Invest, and Check Your Investments Regularly

Make sure you are investing regularly, consistently, and in the best financial vehicles for your goals. But you can't just find an investment adviser, tell him or her what to do, and then assume everything is okay. You must review your investments regularly to make sure they are in line with your risk level, time line, and goals. When your circumstances change, decide if you need to change the types of investments you own. (We'll talk more about investments in chapter 10.) *Automated actions*: Put as much as possible into your retirement plan. (If you're self-employed, utilize a SEP or SIMPLE IRA.) Look at setting up IRAs or Roth IRAs to maximize the tax benefits of your investments. Many banks and investment firms will let you set up an automated investment plan based on *dollar cost averaging*, where you invest a specific amount every single month. Say you wanted to put $50 a month in a particular stock mutual fund. The cost per share of that mutual fund goes up and down depending on the stock market. Let's say this particular mutual fund ranges between $25 and $40 a share on average. Some months, your $50 will buy you 2 shares at $25 each. Some months, your $50 will buy you 1-1/4 shares at $40 each. But over the course of a year, your average cost per share will be higher than $25 and lower than $40. With dollar cost averaging, you usually end up paying less than you would if you had bought shares only when you "thought" they were a good deal. Plus, dollar cost averaging is a great way of investing consistently. *When you should check your progress*: Review your statements monthly, and schedule a time each quarter to review your investments to make sure they are in line with your situation. Meet with your financial adviser to discuss any changes you wish to make.

Path to Success #9: Educate Yourself and Your Family

Make your children's education a priority; and make sure you are investing in keeping your own skills and education current. And educate your children about finances. The best way to give them a secure financial future is to get them used to handling and managing money. Give them an allowance, but insist they set up a bank account with it. Employ them around the house and pay them a set wage for their time and effort. When you teach your children about money—through education, practice, and your own example—you're starting them on the road to financial confidence. *Automated actions*: There are many tax-efficient ways to save for education. See a financial professional to explain the ideal ways to save for college. For yourself, make sure that you pursue ongoing training and skills improvement in your career or profession. (By the way, ongoing professional education is usually a tax-deductible expense. Your tax professional can help you assess what's deductible and what isn't.) Continue your own financial education as well. Keep abreast of financial news, especially about companies and trends that potentially could affect your investments, your job, your local economy, and so on. *When you should check your progress*: Yearly for any education savings; monthly for your general financial education. Make sure to read and/or learn something about finances every week.

Path to Success #10: Transfer Your Wealth to Your Loved Ones Without Creating a Burden for Them

One of the best gifts you can give your family is a legally and financially sound plan that makes your wishes clear, and that transfers to your heirs the greatest amount of your wealth—with the least amount of burden—when you die. *Automated actions*: Wills and trusts are best set up with the advice of an expert—in this case, an estate planning attorney. Depending on your situation, preparing a simple will or trust doesn't have to cost a lot of money, but it can save your family thousands when the time comes and avoid all manner of legal hassles. *When you should check your progress*: Review your estate plan every three years, unless there has been some change to your family or financial status. If that's the case, make sure to update your estate plan immediately.

Remember, the keys to success for any goal are commitment and consistent action. Follow the road map you've created, and re-inspire yourself every day by reviewing your life focus areas, values, and goals. They will help you remember why you are taking the actions that will lead you to success. How much easier is it to invest instead of spending that $50 when you know it's going to help buy you a house in five years, or put your daughter through college? Look at your life focus areas, values, and goals at least once a week to stay excited and motivated. Inspiration and motivation will keep you moving toward *celebration and contribution*—your next step in the confidence cycle.

The Heart of the Matter

➤ Attaining your goals requires commitment. The two keys to commitment are action and consistent follow-through.

➤ To attain your goals faster, you can follow paths to success—specific, tested ways to get from where you are to where you want to be.

➤ One of the most valuable ways to find an effective path to success is by choosing a role model who has accomplished what you want to do.

➤ Once you identify your path to success, you must set in place automatic actions that will lead you along the path.

➤ The best way to build the muscle of consistency is to monitor your progress regularly and compare your progress with your action plan and timeline. Set benchmarks for yourself to evaluate your progress, and set a schedule for your check-ins. If you get off-track, reconnect to the reasons you want this goal, then adjust your approach.

➤ There are 10 key financial paths to success, with associated actions and benchmarks. These paths to success are: get organized; track your expenses; build a cash reserve; have a written plan for your goals; protect yourself from unexpected events; do occupation planning; invest, and check your investments regularly; educate yourself and your family; and transfer your wealth to your loved ones without creating a burden for them.

Kitchen Table Conversation

Ethan and Alice have been married for 10 years. Recently Alice went back to work after their youngest child entered school. Now that they have a second paycheck, they want to maximize their savings for retirement.

Ethan. *Louis, I'm happy you're going to help us save more for our future.*

Alice. *We've been pretty good about putting aside money ever since we got married, but now that I'm back at work we'll have more income each month.*

Ethan. *We've been talking about how much to put into retirement and how much to use for our current needs. Alice could use a better car now that she has to commute, and we have to pay for a babysitter for the kids until we get home.*

Louis. **One of the best things you can do as a couple is to look at what you're currently doing to save for retirement—your path to success—and then figure out how you need to change your actions to reflect Alice's income. Ethan, you've maxed out your contributions to your 401(k) at work, right? Now that there's more coming in from Alice's salary, could you add more of your income into an IRA or a Roth IRA? If you set up this particular path to success now, you should be able to maximize Alice's income while minimizing any taxes.**

Alice. *How about the other things we talked about doing—like getting me a newer car?*

Louis.	*What's more important: the goal of saving more for retirement, or the car?*
Ethan.	*(with a smile) Any way we can have both?*
Louis.	*Of course—but I'd suggest that you do two things. First, put aside as much as you can manage into your retirement plans, and consider whatever your employers match as icing on the cake. Then take a look at whatever money remains and decide if you want to put it toward another goal—your children's education, for instance, or a newer car. Just make sure not to take on a large expenditure until you've got your new level of retirement savings on automatic pilot. I'd suggest waiting at least six months to a year before you make any decision about another car. In fact, do your best to continue living on Ethan's salary, and save Alice's income. That way you can evaluate your new financial situation.*
Ethan.	*I like that plan—it gives us a little time to set up some systems so we don't fritter the extra money away.*
Alice.	*(with a smile) Louis, would it be okay if we used a little of my salary to take our family to a nice restaurant or on an outing once a month?*
Louis.	*(laughs) Of course—but I would suggest setting a limit on how much you spend for your splurge. You both are taking a really smart approach to your new lifestyle. Congratulations!*

8

Step 6: Celebrate and Contribute
Be Grateful and Share What You Have

When you're following the steps of the Confidence Cycle—when you are clear on what's important to you and why, when you have specific goals and the plans to attain them, when you become organized so you know what you already have and what you will need, when you build a team to support your efforts, when you commit and create paths to success and automated actions that help you stay on track, and when you monitor your progress along the way—you stand a much better chance of living a life that is full of meaning, one you can be proud of. But you're not finished yet! The Confidence Cycle concludes with two of the most important aspects of the entire process that all too often we forget or ignore: *celebration and contribution.*

It's easy to get so caught up in the journey that we don't look up and realize we've arrived. Even when we've "made it," we don't make a big deal out of our accomplishments because we're already working on the next goal, task, or project. We finally save the money for the down payment on the house, for instance, but now we're focused on the process of finding a property and putting in an offer. We deposit the last dollar into Junior's college fund, only now we're worried about paying for the next kid's tuition. In this way, we cheat ourselves out of some of the most important moments in our lives. We don't really build confidence because we're always chasing the next thing rather than acknowledging what we've accomplished today. When we don't celebrate our successes we're literally sabotaging our own efforts, because the biggest rewards on our journey have nothing to do with goals and everything to do with emotions.

As you recall, the first step of the Confidence Cycle revolved around motivation, which comes from creating enough positive emotion to keep you moving toward your goals. Well, emotion is just as important at the end as it is in the beginning. Celebration gives you the emotional rewards that will cause you to want to keep pursuing your goals, now and in the future. Celebration is also a great way to involve the people you care about in your goals and outcomes. Some people reach a certain level of success yet find it to be a very lonely experience. When there is no one to share their success, they end up asking, "Is this all there is?" The feeling of success is richer when you know that you have attained all your most important goals while living with purpose and significance, surrounded by people whom you love and who love you. Now, that's a cause for celebration!

What's the best way to ensure that you celebrate your wins? Plan your celebrations in advance. Have you ever planned a party to celebrate a birthday, wedding, anniversary, or other major life event? Isn't the anticipation and fun of planning a great part of the whole experience? And when the party happened, wasn't it great to be surrounded by the people you love? It's the same with planning your goal achievement celebrations. Having that to look forward to, and the anticipation of sharing your success with the people you love, will make the journey toward your goals more pleasurable. However, make sure you don't just celebrate at the end of the process. Instead, have *mini-celebrations* along the way as you reach the benchmarks you set for yourself. When you go to the gym consistently for a month, for instance, you could treat yourself to a new workout outfit, or try the new healthy restaurant in your neighborhood. When you save a certain amount toward retirement, have a "pre-retirement" party. Even simple rewards and celebrations—like cards, outings, an afternoon at the beach or in the woods, and so on—can help keep you motivated to do more toward your goals. In fact, I believe you should never move on to a new goal in any area until you have celebrated the goal you have just achieved. When you give yourself the chance to pat yourself on the back, and to share your success and joy with the people you love, then you'll not only enjoy the destination but you'll also enjoy the process of getting there.

Here are some questions to guide you in setting up your celebrations.

1. **How will you celebrate your success when you achieve this goal?** Make sure to do something that you will truly enjoy and can anticipate with pleasure. Do you want to throw a party? Give yourself something special? Take a vacation or a break? Whatever your celebration, make sure it has meaning for you.

2. **Whom do you want to include?** Sharing a celebration with those we love makes it truly special. You might want to invite those who helped you with this particular goal, or just those whose lives have touched you along the way.

3. **What mini-celebrations can you plan when you hit the benchmarks you set up in Step 5?** Make sure every celebration makes you feel really great about your efforts while keeping you motivated to continue your progress.

Congratulations! You have taken what was once a dream and turned it into a tangible reality. You are among the very few in this world who take action instead of wasting time in excuses. You are ready for the last, most important aspects of the Confidence Cycle: gratitude and contribution. These are at the core of any real, ongoing success, and will give your achievements more meaning and help you expand beyond your current goals.

Lasting Confidence Comes from Gratitude and Contribution

Even as you pursue goals to make your life better, you should be grateful for what you have. Instead of looking at someone else and saying, "Why aren't I successful like he/she is?" take a moment to appreciate the gifts you possess. All of us can get so wrapped up in looking at what we don't have that we can forget the amazing gifts we have already received. Life. Health. Family. Whatever level of abundance we enjoy. When we remember to be grateful for whatever we have in our lives, even if it's less than we may want or need, we open ourselves up emotionally for the kinds of positive emotions that will make us feel successful and wealthy no matter what. Gratitude is the ultimate secret of abundance, and the antidote to scarcity thinking. When we focus on gratitude and abundance, instead of being envious and jealous of the success of others, we regard their success as a pathway we can follow in our pursuit of our own goals. All it takes is a little skill, a little patience, a little hard work—and the belief that we are ready to make our own success.

Strangely enough, you'll feel more grateful, and your goals will have more meaning, if you contribute to something larger than yourself. Contribution can help motivate you and keep you in touch with feelings of gratitude and abundance. If you are saving for retirement, what if you donated a small amount each year to an organization like Meals on Wheels that takes care of older people with limited resources? How much better would you feel about saving when you know you are helping others with your money as well as yourself? You also could contribute to the other people in your life. Say your goal has been to get a promotion, and your action plan included a project you undertook with several coworkers. Your efforts were successful, and you got your promotion. You could combine celebration and contribution by throwing a party for the team that worked on the project, or acknowledge your team in other ways. Contribution links your goals with the larger world; it creates a legacy and expands the impact of your success far beyond personal gain.

I was the first person in my immediate family to go to college, and when I attended UCLA I participated in the university's Partnership Program. We would bring to the campus students who might never have thought of attending college—kids from the disadvantaged neighborhoods where no one ever talked about higher education—and show them what a university environment is like. I asked the people who were running the program if I could bring my little brother when I hosted some students from East Los Angeles (where I grew up). I taught my brother everything I had learned about making the transition to the world of college. My brother followed in my footsteps and went to college. Today he's a high school guidance counselor in Los Angeles and wants to become a principal. I'm proud of what my brother has done, and happy that I was able to contribute to his life. Through the years I've continued to support kids from disadvantaged neighborhoods to understand that they, too, can graduate from high school and go on to college or university. By helping these kids I give back in gratitude for what I've been able to accomplish. By tying the achievement of your goals to something beyond yourself, you give them greater meaning. But just as you should plan your celebrations in advance, start thinking now about how you can give back as you work toward your goals.

For each goal, ask yourself the following.

1. **Who else will you contribute to with this goal?** Make a list of the people and organizations that could be touched by your success. If your goal is to lose weight, who else will benefit? Your family, because you'll be healthier? Your friends, who might see you as a role model? Maybe you could tie your weight loss to a regular contribution to a charity or group whose work you value, like your church or the Red Cross or the homeless. Every individual or organization who benefits from your goal will give you another reason to reach it—and another reason to celebrate when you do.

2. **What kind of contribution will you make?** Planning the contributions you will make can encourage you to stay on track in the tough times. Say that your goal is to get a job after being out of work for a while. You decide that when you land a job you'll volunteer at the local job bank one Saturday a month, counseling others who are looking for work. Your volunteering is both inspirational and practical, and can be a valuable contribution that makes a difference. What kind of contribution would inspire and assist others?

3. **How will you remember to feel grateful, not just when you reach a benchmark or accomplish a goal, but every day?** The simple act of looking for something each day to be grateful for will help you stay on track even in the toughest times, or when your progress toward your goals isn't as rapid as you would like. Take a few moments before you get out of bed in the morning, or before you go to sleep at night, to ask yourself, "What am I grateful for today?" Keep asking the question until you find something to be grateful for. When you actively search for things to be grateful for in your life, you'll be surprised at how rich you can feel regardless of circumstances.

Building Confidence in Finances and in Life

All work—indeed, all life—consists of setting goals, working towards their attainment, developing greater confidence in your abilities, and then setting newer, higher goals. The Confidence Cycle is designed not simply to help you produce results in your life, but also to help you build the most important result of all: greater confidence in yourself and your ability to take charge of your future. This cycle is an upward spiral, as each goal carries you to a higher level of achievement. Every time you attain a goal or make progress toward it, you are building the confidence that will give you the courage to take on bigger challenges, which will produce bigger results.

This upward spiral of confidence is equally important in your financial life. I hope you've figured out by now that everyone's version of financial confidence will be a little bit different, depending on the life focus areas, values, and goals he or she has. I may feel I have arrived when I have a nice house in a good neighborhood, a solid marriage, enough money in the bank to put my kids through college and to provide for retirement. For my cousin, it might be a business worth $3 million, a big house and a vacation home. Everyone is different—but somehow, we all have a sense when we've arrived at the place we call financial confidence. Once we develop that mindset, taking the actions to create the lives we desire becomes easy. We know where we want to go, why we wish to do so, and how to get there. Then it's just a matter of taking actions through time to make our dreams real.

But how do we *know* when we have arrived at our destination of both financial confidence and life success? When we take a trip somewhere we know when we have arrived usually because there is a signpost telling us so. What are the signs you will receive when you arrive at your own "destination"? The truest signs will not be external, like a big house, a successful business, or money in the bank. Instead, they will be internal: how you feel about yourself and your life. You will know you have arrived when you experience peace of mind, happiness, joy, abundance, and confidence. At first these feelings may be momentary flashes of content amidst your efforts; but eventually you'll feel more and more happiness as you pursue your goals. In truth, financial confidence has far less to do with what you have, and far more to do with who you become. When you are living the life you designed, and you have created a financial base that allows you to pursue the dreams that have meaning for you and those you love, then you will experience financial confidence as it is meant to be felt.

In truth, confidence isn't really a destination; it is a process. You don't "reach" confidence; you "become" confident. And when you are confident, you know that every goal contains within it the seeds of an even greater dream. The secret of confidence on My Street is always to raise the bar, for yourself and for what you believe you can achieve. Certainly, you've got to enjoy what you accomplish or you'll never want to achieve even more. But those who understand true confidence know how to celebrate and enjoy their success even as they look forward to the next step.

The My Street Money Confidence Cycle is the same process that I go through with people on My Street to help them achieve success and have happy, fulfilling lives along the way. Does it take some work? Of course. But haven't you noticed that when you put effort into achieving a goal and then see that effort pay off, you feel a greater sense of satisfaction and accomplishment than you would if you'd gotten your goal handed to you on a silver platter? In truth, confidence and success are built not from our results but from our efforts. Remember a moment in your life when you were successful through your own efforts? The knowledge that you achieved that success by working for it made the success even sweeter, and made your efforts seem worthwhile. When we work toward a goal and achieve it, we gain the result *plus* knowledge and experience—which are often more valuable than the result itself. But here's the bottom line: to build the confidence you need to succeed on My Street, you have to be willing to go through the cycle. You must put its six steps into practice regularly. When you do so, you'll not only reach your goals, but you'll also be able to evaluate your progress and enjoy watching your confidence growing stronger and stronger. And once you've built your confidence, you can use the same process to gain results in other areas of life and with other goals.

Recently I heard of a study on muscle memory—it stated that once you build a muscle through consistent effort and demand, that muscle will retain a "memory" in its cells of the level of strength it attained. And even if you cease to work out for a while and the muscle gets flabby, you can regain your former level of strength far more easily, simply because you once built up that muscle. I believe that our confidence "muscles" also have a very strong "memory." Once we put in consistent effort to pursue our goals, and we achieve success in one area, even when we experience setbacks in life our confidence muscle can rebound quickly, as long as we are willing to get back into the gym and put in the effort once again.

In today's world, where so many of us have gone through difficult times and a lot of setbacks, we need to take heart and remember: if we've succeeded once, we can do so again. The challenges we face may be daunting, and the goals we seek may seem very far away. But every day we can make the choice: to keep working, a little bit at a time, toward making things better, or to stop trying, give up, and continue to lose more and more ground. Life never stands still; as someone once said, every day you're either growing or dying. And it's always your choice as to which direction you want to take your life. I'm here to tell you that by continuing to pursue your goals, you are building the "muscle" that will serve you well in the long run.

The Ultimate Destination

Imagine it's a beautiful spring day, and you're going somewhere special. You walk into a tastefully decorated room, with thick carpet and plush drapes. Soft music is playing in the background. You look around and you see all the people who know and love you. Then you notice a large wooden rectangular box against one wall of this room. It's a coffin. You walk toward the coffin, look inside—and see yourself. You're at your own funeral. Everyone sits down, and then one by one, people stand up and talk about you. They are completely honest; they talk about your good and bad points. They share every detail of your life, including how they felt about you. What do they say? If your funeral were held tomorrow, how would people describe your life so far? If it happened 30 years in the future, how would you like them to talk about your life: your accomplishments, your relationships, how you were loved, what you contributed?

This mental exercise is a great reminder of your final destination. No matter what road you take—whether you make it to financial confidence or get stuck in struggle and survival—we all end up at the same point. What truly matters is what we do with our lives before those eulogies are delivered. And that is completely and utterly up to each of us. Each person builds his or her own destiny, and the end of the journey is determined by each choice we make along the way.

You have to decide how you're going to live each day and then live it as best you can, according to the design you have created for yourself. You can't let circumstances dictate your dreams or hinder your efforts. When you know you are living a life in which you are following your dreams, and those dreams make life better not only for you but also for those you love on My Street, in your community, and perhaps even the world as a whole, then somehow the end of the road looks a whole lot brighter. Your eulogy will be filled with love and appreciation for a life that made a difference. And you can look on with pride and great peace of mind, knowing the world is better for your having spent time on it.

I hope you will use the Confidence Cycle to start your own journey to success and happiness on My Street. But more than that, I hope you will find as many ways as you can to enjoy every step. I challenge you to use the creativity and energy God has given each of us to turn your journey to confidence into a pilgrimage of discovery, laughter, and joy. When you can pursue each of your goals with excitement, when you attack even the most difficult tasks with enthusiasm, when you keep your commitments to yourself and others with a smile on your face and happiness in your heart, and yes, when you overcome those natural moments of laziness or fear or discouragement by keeping the pleasure of reaching your ultimate goal in your thoughts, and when you expand outside your own small concerns to be grateful and to contribute to others, then your journey will enrich you far more than any material riches you may accumulate along the way. Your success and happiness on My Street will be assured, because your external wealth will simply be a reflection of the greater treasures you have inside.

The Heart of the Matter

➤ Celebration, gratitude, and contribution are some of the most important parts of the Confidence Cycle. We need to celebrate our wins, be grateful for what we have, and contribute to something outside of ourselves.

➤ Plan your celebrations in advance, and don't wait until you achieve your goal; instead, plan mini-celebrations for the benchmarks along the way. Share your celebrations with other people.

➤ Gratitude is the antidote to scarcity thinking, and contributing to something greater than yourself will keep you motivated.

➤ The Confidence Cycle is an upward spiral, where each goal carries you to a higher level of achievement.

➤ Financial confidence is a mindset based on a clear vision of who you want to become. You'll know when you've attained financial confidence when you feel abundant and you experience peace of mind and happiness.

Kitchen Table Conversation

Matthew, an entrepreneur, wanted to develop a plan to increase his dry cleaning business.

Matthew. *Louis, my dry cleaning business has been doing well and we opened another store recently. But I want to grow my current business by 50 percent in the next two years and then add three new locations.*

Louis. **That's an ambitious goal, Matthew. How are you doing on your other life focus areas? Have you looked at them lately?**

Matthew. *Quite honestly, for the past year or so I've only focused on the business. My wife understands—in fact, she runs one store while I spend most of my time in the other.*

Louis. **On a scale of 1 to 10, 1 being little or nothing and 10 being great, how would you rate your level of intimacy with your wife?**

Matthew. *(uncomfortable) Probably a 3, maybe a 2.*

Louis. **How about your health? When was the last time you saw a doctor?**

Matthew. *In January—he commented on my putting on some extra weight and not getting any exercise. And he did say my blood pressure was too high, and also my stress level.*

Louis. **When you opened your second store, did you acknowledge your accomplishment and celebrate your success?**

Matthew. *No—we were too busy getting it open.*

Louis.	*Matthew, I understand how excited you are by the goal of increasing your business by 50 percent. But I'd like you to try something. Close your eyes and imagine it's two years from now. You've succeeded in opening three new stores. How do you feel?*
Matthew.	(his eyes closed) Like a business tycoon!
Louis.	*With your eyes closed, look down at your body. Have you taken care of your health for the last two years?*
Matthew.	No…. In fact, I've put on another 10 pounds.
Louis.	*What do you think your life expectancy would be at that point?*
Matthew.	I don't want to think about it.
Louis.	*But you need to think about it, if you want to be around. Now, imagine looking over at your wife. You've spent two more years not paying any attention to her because you've both been working so hard. Do you feel closer to her?*
Matthew.	(with a sigh) No. She looks tired and sad.
Louis.	*Matthew, I see a lot of people who put their business or career ahead of everything else, and forget that other aspects of life are a lot more important in the long run. Business and financial success is only a part of the legacy you'll leave after you're gone. What else would you like to have as your legacy?*
Matthew.	A loving family. Kids. A great relationship. Feeling that my life mattered. I want to make sure that my family is well taken care of while I'm here and after I'm gone.

Louis.   *Is it possible that you may need to put as much effort and time into yourself and your relationship as you do into your business?*

Matthew.   *You're right. I have to take care of both my wife and my health if I want to keep them both for a long time.*

Louis.   *One more thing I'd suggest to enrich your life: find a cause or place you can contribute to others, outside of your immediate family or business. Where would you like to contribute?*

Matthew.   *My first job was in the neighborhood dry cleaner's, and my boss, Mr. Drucker, took the time to teach me everything he knew about being a successful small businessman. Perhaps I can take some kids into my business and do for them what Mr. Drucker did for me.*

Louis.   *Now, imagine that it's two years from now. You've been working on your business but you've also been taking care of your health and your relationship, and you've been helping young people start on the path to entrepreneurship. How do you feel?*

Matthew.   *Happy beyond belief. I'm thinner and fitter, my blood pressure's normal, and I have tons of energy. My wife and I have a great relationship, and we have a beautiful son. I've got several young people working in the store, and others that I've mentored are going off to college to study business. I have more than enough money to support my family and grow my business, but I also have time to spend with Molly and our boy. Thanks, Louis. That's the real life of my dreams.*

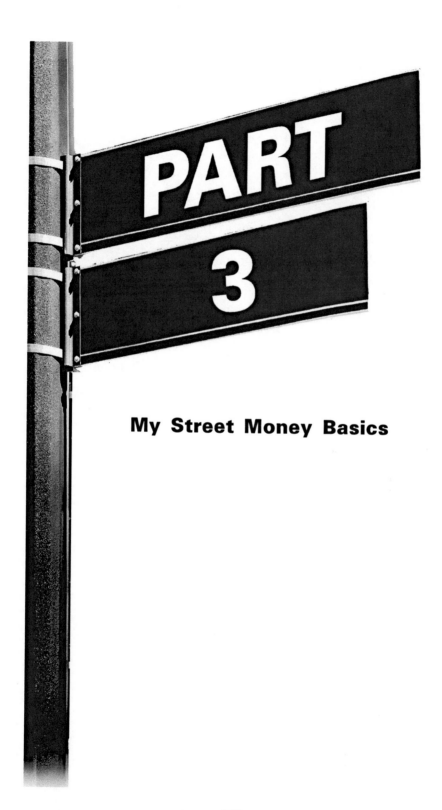

PART

3

My Street Money Basics

It's pretty clear that one of the problems people have had over the last few years is that they stopped trying to follow a few basic guidelines—like using credit intelligently, only signing contracts they understand, living within their means and not taking on too much debt, and so on. Granted, many people were given a lot of bad advice by financial salespeople, the media, government institutions, bad lenders, etc.; and they may have found themselves stuck in financial dilemmas that weren't completely of their making—like watching the value of their retirement accounts or home drop by 30 to 50 percent. However, I can say with certainty there are ways to educate yourself on financial basics that will help insulate you from the worst effects of the economic storms that come up every several years. And make no mistake: there will be more economic storms ahead. Like nature (and our lives), economies have patterns and cycles that recur, and you need to be ready to cope with the storms and take advantage of the sunshine when it reappears.

In this section we're going to talk about what I call "My Street Money Basics": basic principles that will help you through some of the bigger financial storms of our changing economy, and provide you shelter from the smaller financial storms created by unscrupulous people, bad investment choices, and mistakes caused by a lack of knowledge. I believe the fundamental principles outlined in the Confidence Cycle will help you take advantage of the good times and make it easier to weather the bad. And when you add a little clarity about financial basics, you'll be able to protect what you have and make better decisions about the ways to handle your money now and in the future.

To help people remember the fundamentals of building or rebuilding the financial confidence they need to live happily on My Street, I use the acronym S.A.V.E., which represents the four financial basics.

S = Solid foundation. This includes such elements as an emergency cash reserve, the right insurance, a good credit rating, a monthly budget or spending plan, tax planning, a retirement plan, and estate planning.

A = Automated investing. I'll say it again: saving and investing a certain amount each month automatically is the best way to build your confidence as well as your bank account.

V = Variety in your investments. In chapter 10 we'll talk about the power of investing in different assets (CDs and money markets, stocks, bonds, real estate, and so on) so you can better protect yourself from the ups and downs of the economy.

E = Educate yourself about money. You need to become comfortable with the basics of financial planning as well as the language of money. A good, solid understanding of the essentials will help you care for you and your family.

In this section we're going to focus on "E," educating yourself about money, and we'll cover some of the essentials of credit, contracts, and investing. I hope this will provide a good grounding so that you can handle yourself financially with more confidence, and use this as a launching point to learn more about finances. (There is a lot of great information that goes into more detail on financial planning; you can find a list that I recommend at www.louisbarajas.com.)

Building financial confidence in My Street is simple, but it does take time—and I can assure you that it will be time well spent. In fact, the best investment you can make in your financial future right now is time. In previous chapters we talked a little about the power of compounding, how a small amount of money invested for a long period increases dramatically. In just the same way, the time you invest now in creating a solid financial future will compound to help you create a secure and happy life. You also will accrue the dividends of peace of mind and confidence that you are taking care of yourself and those you love. It will help you and your family to live happily on My Street for many years to come.

9

Basics #1: Use Credit Wisely, Read and Understand Contracts Before You Sign

Almost everyone will use credit at some point in their lives—to buy a car, to purchase a home, or simply for the convenience of not having to carry cash for everyday purchases. However, many people nowadays use debit cards for purchases and pay cash for everything they can. This is a pretty good strategy for making sure you don't live beyond your means, and it may be a great strategy if you have abused your credit in the past. But in order to do almost anything financially in the U.S., whether it's buying a car or purchasing a home to starting a business, you're going to need to learn to handle credit responsibly. Especially today, lenders want to see that you can handle a small amount of credit before they'll give you access to larger amounts for cars or home purchases. And if you've messed up your finances in the past, with a bankruptcy, a series of late payments, or having too much credit for the amount of income you make, then it's even more important to re-establish your ability to handle credit well. And to do this, you must understand the basics of credit.

The good news is that many financial institutions are encouraging, if not requiring, people to learn to manage credit before they can borrow money. The days of being able to get a $10,000-limit credit card while you're in college, or borrowing 125 percent of the purchase price of a home so you don't have to put down any kind of a down payment, are pretty much over. While this may have been fun while it lasted, it was like a fraternity drinking binge—lots of immediate drunken pleasure followed by immense and lasting pain of a serious (fiscal) hangover. And like frat boys who drank too much and then trashed the dean's house, causing the dean to punish the entire fraternity, today we're all suffering from the consequences of the irresponsible actions of the folks who binged financially when they couldn't handle their "liquor"—i.e. their debt. So, we're all on the wagon as far as debt is concerned. It's tough to get a loan even if your credit is good. And if you lose your job, or owe more on your house than it's worth, or you overspend on your credit cards and are barely making the minimum payment, you are probably in a lot of financial pain. It's still possible to rebound and get credit even in today's market—but first, you have to prove that you can be fiscally responsible.

To master credit, you need two things: (1) some basic understanding of terms, and (2) a few guidelines to help you make the most of your credit. Let's start with the definitions of credit, credit report, and credit score.

Understanding Credit, Your Credit Report, and Your Credit Score

"Credit" essentially means that someone—an institution (like a bank, finance or mortgage company, or department store) or person (like your Uncle Bob who loans you $2,000 to buy a car)—gives you a sum of money and asks you to pay it back over a certain period of time. However, you must pay interest each month for the privilege of using the borrowed funds. In your Uncle Bob's case, he may only charge you 5 percent a year, or $100 on that $2,000 debt. In the case of auto loans or mortgages, interest rates can range from a low of 5 percent to a high of 20 percent depending on your credit score. With credit cards, the yearly interest rate on your outstanding balance can be anywhere from 10 percent or more. And if you miss even one payment on a credit card, you could end up paying as much as 30 percent in interest. (See the "Do's and Don'ts of Credit" below.)

Every debt you incur is noted on your *credit report*—the financial records on each of us that are kept by local and national credit bureaus. A credit report is basically a shortcut for lenders to use when deciding whether to loan you money or give you a credit card. Three major credit reporting bureaus—Experian, TransUnion, and Equifax—gather information from smaller agencies and compile them to create a credit report on you. Your credit report contains past and present financial information, such as:

» Personal information like your name, address, Social Security number, birth date, and current and past employers

» Financial information, including the amount of credit you currently have, including credit card accounts, store credit accounts, auto loan, mortgage, lines of credit, (any debt that is held by an institution—Uncle Bob's loan won't be listed), and your monthly payments on any outstanding debts. Your credit report also shows how much credit you've used and how much is available to you. For example, if you have three credit cards with credit limits of $10,000 each, that means you would have $30,000 in total available credit, assuming you don't owe anything currently on those cards. However, if your current balances on those three cards are $9,000 each, you would have only $3,000 in available credit.

» Payment history, especially any late or missed payments on any loan or balance. Any loans, cards, or accounts that have been closed also will show up on your credit report.

Other items that show up include information from public records that could affect your creditworthiness, like tax liens, bankruptcies, collections, and court judgments (awards of damages for example); official requests for your credit report from potential lenders (too many inquiries can make a lender think you're getting in over your head debt-wise); and any disputes you may have filed with the credit reporting bureau about items on the report.

Unfortunately, mistakes do occur on your credit report. You may have made a payment that for some reason the lender didn't record on time and it shows up on your credit report as a late or missed payment. Or someone steals your identity, opens credit cards using your name and Social Security number, and charges a bunch of stuff before you're aware of the theft. Since lenders, employers, and insurance companies all look at your credit report these days, it's absolutely essential to check your credit report at least once a year, and to dispute any mistakes you may find. On my website, www. louisbarajas.com, you'll find the contact information for the three major credit reporting bureaus, as well as information on how to file a dispute.

As you've probably discovered if you've ever applied for a car loan or home mortgage, banks and lending institutions use an even shorter version of your credit report to decide whether to even consider lending you money, and at what rate of interest. This shorter version, which boils down your creditworthiness to a three-digit number, is your *credit score* (also known as your FICO™ score). This number, which ranges between 300 (terrible) and 850 (super), is supposed to predict with some accuracy whether you will repay a loan reliably—in other words, how much of a risk the bank or lending institution is taking if they give you a loan. The more risk you represent, the higher interest you'll be charged, if the bank or loan company will lend to you at all.

Each credit reporting bureau comes up with its own number for your credit score (don't ask why; the way credit bureaus come up with your credit score is based upon proprietary formulas, so there's no way for the average person to figure it out). However, each credit bureau takes into account:

» Your payment history (even one late or missed payment can lower your credit score)

» Any outstanding debt—how much money you already owe, and any new debts you've taken on (for example, getting a car loan or new credit card will reduce your credit score for a short time)

» How long you've had credit (if you've been handling credit successfully for 10 years, you're a better risk than if you just got your first credit card), and the kinds of credit you have (credit cards, mortgage, installment loans, etc.)

» Inquiries from other lending institutions about your credit-worthiness

In the same way that many people (landlords, employers, and insurers) are checking your credit report these days to decide whether to do business with you, they also can check your credit score. That's why it's so important for you to know your credit score, make sure your credit report has no mistakes on it that can lower your score, and do what you can to raise your credit score.

The Do's and Don'ts of Mastering Credit

Here are the most important do's and don'ts of establishing, or re-establishing, your ability to manage credit and build a stellar credit history starting today.

» *DO establish credit and use it responsibly.* The first step to using credit responsibly is to establish some. That means getting some kind of loan or credit card and making regular, on-time payments for several months. If you've had problems with credit in the past, it might be hard to get a credit card or loan at anything approaching a reasonable interest rate. However, there are ways to establish a credit record even when your current credit rating is bad. Some banks offer a "credit card" that's essentially a debit card. You deposit a certain amount—$300, for example—in a savings account, and then you can charge up to that amount on your card. The card is guaranteed by your savings, and you gain the benefit of building good credit when you make regular payments.

Another option to re-establish credit is to have someone with good credit co-sign a loan with you. However, this can be very difficult if you ever default on the loan, as your co-signer then becomes responsible for the entire debt. You'd better be completely committed to making all the loan payments on time and in full; otherwise, having someone co-sign a loan for you can create a great deal of pain, both financially and in your relationship with the co-signer.

Always remember the reasons for credit: (1) the convenience of not having to carry much cash, (2) the ability to pay for large purchases (house, car, etc.) over a period of time, (3) establishing a record of you as a solid, responsible financial citizen who will take care of the bank's money (which you are borrowing when you take out a loan to buy a car or house) and provide them with a guaranteed return. The way you build this financial "identity" with lenders is to handle small amounts of credit responsibly.

» *DO look at the total amount of the debt, not the monthly payment.* I see people run into trouble with this frequently—especially when they are buying a car. A young couple walks into the dealership looking for a good, used, family car for about $10,000, but then the salesperson shows them an almost-new SUV and says, "You can have this for exactly the same monthly payment as you would for that four-year-old mini-van!" What the salesperson *doesn't* point out is that the SUV will cost them over $21,000 including interest, and instead of paying off the mini-van in three years the couple will be paying for the SUV for six. Worse yet, the more debt you have in proportion to your income, the less likely you are to be able to borrow any more money. If this young couple wants to buy a house, for example, that big auto loan might count against them and make it harder for them to get a mortgage.

Most salespeople tell you how much you'll spend per month rather than telling you the final cost of the item, which may be a lot more than you can actually afford. Plus, some installment loans arranged by sellers can be for much higher interest rates than you'd have on a credit card. Be careful when it comes to making big purchases; make sure you know exactly (1) the total amount that you'll pay, *including* interest, (2) the interest rate of the loan and the terms, and (3) how many months it will take to pay off the purchase. (By the way, all of these things should be spelled out in the purchase agreement, or contract; read the section on contracts in this chapter for some important ways to protect yourself before you sign any agreement.)

» *DO pay your bills on time, every time.* Every late payment on a bill gets noted on your credit report and counts against you when credit bureaus and lenders evaluate your creditworthiness and calculate your credit score. However, you'll also experience more *immediate* financial pain, as nowadays many credit card companies and lending institutions charge high fees for each late payment, and they can raise the interest rate on your card or loan to the default rate (which can be 28 percent and up) after just one missed payment. If you have a problem remembering to pay your bills on time, many banks will allow you to pay by telephone or to set up automatic and/ or online bill pay through your checking account. Whatever strategy you use, paying your bills on time every time will help you keep your credit record clean and strong.

» *DO protect your creditworthiness.* Check your credit record regularly. People make mistakes, but so do banks, credit card companies, and merchants. If you find a mistake on your credit record, take it up with the bank, store, or lending institution that made the mistake. You also can lodge a protest with the credit bureau, or have them put a note in your file explaining the incident. And *never* allow others to use your credit. Protect your credit cards, bank account numbers, Social Security number, and so on. Your credit record is your financial reputation—and once it's damaged, you can spend a lifetime cleaning it up. Put your effort into protecting your credit record from the start, and you'll find your road to financial success will be much smoother.

» *DO know your credit score. If it's low, do what's necessary to raise it.* You can check your credit reports with all three of the big credit bureaus (Experian, Equifax, and TransUnion) once a year for free at www.annualcreditreport.com, and for a small additional fee you also can see your current credit score. It used to be that you could get a favorable rate on an auto loan or home mortgage with a credit score in the high 600s. But with the tightening of credit requirements and lower availability of loans, you need a score of 740 or higher to qualify for the best rates. What should you do to raise your credit score? Pay your bills on time, every time. Correct any errors on your credit report. Don't close any old credit accounts (part of your credit score is based on how long you've had credit) or open any new ones (new credit lines will temporarily lower your score). Make sure to keep your balances on credit cards below 20 percent of your credit lines. And unless absolutely necessary, don't give permission for too many lenders, employers, or institutions to check your credit score. Each inquiry within a short period of time raises a red flag for potential lenders, who will assume you are looking to take on more debt than you can handle.

If you apply for a loan or credit card and are turned down due to a low credit score, ask the lender to show you a copy of the documentation provided by the credit bureau that lists the reasons for your low score. It'll make your job of raising your credit score easier as you will know exactly where the problem lies.

» *DON'T mistake a credit limit for the amount of money you can spend.* For many years, credit card companies were issuing cards with ridiculously high credit limits on them. People would get the cards and think to themselves, *Wow! A $10,000 limit! Now I can buy the furniture, go on vacation, and treat my family to some really nice gifts.* They would forget that they were making $40,000 a year and spending $38,000 on food, shelter, transportation, taxes, and so on. And unless they pay off their entire credit card bill each month, they're not just spending $10,000; they're also spending the amount of interest the bank is charging them for the privilege of using that money. They'd also forget that every dollar they put on their credit card is a dollar they aren't saving or investing. Instead of saving for the future, they would be paying off credit card bills for years. Don't mortgage your financial future to buy nonessential luxuries today. Your credit limit is the amount of credit you *can* use, not that you *should* use. Remember that a portion of your credit score is determined by how much credit you have available and unused. Keep an eye on your balances and even if you can't pay off your credit balances each month, do what you can to keep the balances below 20 percent of your credit limit.

» *DON'T get caught in the minimum monthly payment trap.* Did you know that with most credit cards, paying only the minimum monthly payment will keep you from paying off that debt for years, while the interest keeps adding up and up? Here's an example. Say you have a balance of $5,000 on a credit card that charges 15 percent interest. Your minimum monthly payment is 4 percent of the total amount owed on the card—$200 the first month, and slightly less each month as you pay off the balance. But the problem is that your payment barely covers the interest you're being charged and leaves very little to apply to the principal of $5,000. If you charge nothing else on the card and keep making only the minimum payment each month, it will take you 10 years and 3 months to pay off the balance, and you'll be charged $2,180 in interest. You'll pay $7,180 to cover a $5,000 debt!

Paying only the minimum is a trap that you must get out of immediately. But there are three real secrets to getting out of the minimum payment trap. First, stop charging anything until you pay off the debt you already have. Second, set up a plan to pay off your credit card debt in a reasonable amount of time. (On www.louisbarajas.com I have a form called the Debt Dissolver that can help you organize your payments by paying off your highest interest cards first.) Third, once you've paid off your debt, never pay just the minimum unless you are caught in dire financial circumstances, like losing a job or an unexpected medical or family emergency. Even paying as little as $10 a month more than the minimum payment can make a big difference in the amount of time it takes you to pay off the balance and the amount of interest you'll end up paying.

» *DON'T borrow more than your current earnings will allow you to repay in a reasonable amount of time.* Remember that family who went into the car dealership and got talked into buying a $21,000 SUV instead of an inexpensive mini-van? Let's assume that their yearly income was $45,000, and their monthly payment on the car was $300—manageable, you might think. But what if this family also had three or four credit cards with limits of $5,000 to $10,000 each, and they were using those cards up to the limit? They'd end up with minimum monthly payments of $500 or more total on the credit cards, in addition to the car loan payment of $300. But what if, after they paid for rent or mortgage, food, health insurance, utilities, and gas, they only had $200 a month left to cover the $800 a month they owe on credit card bills and car payment? They would fall further behind each month because they failed to live according to their income. Remember, the real goal of credit is *not* to finance a lifestyle above your means. It's to have access to money when you need it for big purchases like cars and homes—things that you will need to pay off over time. It's also useful to have access to credit for emergencies (although if you are following a monthly savings plan, you should have some cash set aside for that). Before you make any purchase on credit, you'd better be sure it's something you can pay for easily based on your current income.

Managing credit responsibly means knowing how much your monthly expenses are and making sure that you can pay off any debts with what's left of your current income while you save a certain amount for emergencies and future needs like retirement or your children's education. You must set up a spending plan that states your total monthly income, your total expenses (including monthly savings and investment), and how much extra income you have left each month. Remember, however, "discretionary income" is not a target to be spent monthly; it's just how much money you have available either to spend or to save toward a big purchase down the road. When you're clear on exactly where your money goes each month, and you have the certainty you are living within your means—that is, spending less than your current income—you'll have a peace of mind and sense of enjoyment that money cannot buy.

Think of credit as a way of using a relatively small amount of money to learn big lessons, and to prove to the financial establishment that you can be trusted to handle money responsibly. When you have learned to use credit wisely, it can be a wonderful tool to allow you to make major purchases, like a house or an auto. Used unwisely, credit is just like a drug, enabling bad behavior and creating more problems both today and tomorrow. Credit is a fact of life on My Street, and you're much better off learning to use it well.

Dealing with Contracts

All of us at one time or another will have some sort of contract stuck under our noses and be told, "Sign here." It could be an application for a loan, or a credit card, could be a promissory note, or a lease for your first apartment, or an agreement to purchase furniture. Most people scan the document, try to understand as much of it as possible, and then sign it immediately, hoping that everything is okay. That's a sure recipe for financial hardship. Instead, you must spend a few moments to master the basics of contracts. Understand that most contracts are for your protection as much as for the other person's. If you master a few simple elements and, most important, are willing to ask questions, then contracts can be a powerful tool that will help you ensure a better financial future.

Building financial confidence means that you must stop being intimidated by written agreements. In fact, you need to learn to *insist* on having them. If it isn't written, it isn't real. Even if it's a few lines written on a scrap of paper saying, "On such-and-such a date, I will pay my cousin $10,000 for his car, a three-year-old Chevy sedan," that scrap of paper can save you a lot of grief in the long run. If there's something you don't understand in any contract, ask for explanations. And you must *never* sign anything until you are absolutely clear about what is said in the contract, what the terms are, and what you are agreeing to do. Remember, building or rebuilding your finances will inevitably bring more complicated transactions, more legal and financial agreements, and more contracts. You need to learn to understand and use contracts effectively now so you can handle them successfully in the future. Luckily, taking a few simple precautions could save you years of financial pain and stress, and help you rebuild both your financial confidence and your financial health at the same time. Here are three keys to keep in mind when dealing with contracts.

Key #1: You must understand any contract that you encounter. If you don't understand it, don't sign it.

Most people hate dealing with the legal and financial terms in contracts because they don't understand them. It's like being in a foreign country not speaking the language—only in this case, not speaking the language can cost you a lot. But if you've ever learned a new language, you know it can be difficult at first, but after a very short time the new language becomes much easier. Contracts are written in a language that's unfamiliar to most of us, but once you understand a few key words, you can comprehend the meaning with a lot more confidence. However, if you look at a contract and tell yourself, "I'll never understand this," you're right. You've got to think, "I can learn this. I'm committed to mastering this because it is important. I'll do whatever it takes to understand what I'm agreeing to." With that attitude, a contract becomes an opportunity to be seized rather than an obstacle to be overcome.

Some people don't want to take the time to read over a contract because they're afraid they will look stupid, or unknowledgeable, or they're feeling pressured by the person offering the deal. But the only thing that's really stupid is not taking the time to read a contract thoroughly. Ask to take a copy of the agreement home so you can review it. If the salesperson or whoever says no, get up and walk out. No respectable businessperson will balk at letting you review a contract for at least 24 hours; in fact, he or she should appreciate your desire to know what you are signing. If necessary, consult an attorney to ensure the contract is written fairly.

Key #2: Own your power: It's your money/time/decision.

Even though it may not always seem so, as the client you ultimately have the power in the interaction. You're the one who is going
to spend the money (and be responsible for paying the money back).
If it's an employment application or contract, you're the one commit-
ting to fulfill the agreement. However, when dealing with contracts
most of us feel the other side has the power and smarts, and we don't.
That's a lie. A contract is an agreement reached between two people/
entities/institutions. Your side has just as much clout as theirs does if
you will step up and take it. You have the right—indeed, the responsibility—to understand the terms of the agreement before you sign
anything.

Even though it can be very tough to walk away when you've spent
several hours at a dealership haggling over a car or working with an
attorney on a business arrangement, don't let yourself be pressured
emotionally into something that goes against your best interests. If
the deal isn't right, no matter how sweet the car or the business arrangement may seem, ultimately it will not serve your best interests.
You have to be willing to stand your ground, say no, and walk away.
Be warned, however: Once you sign a contract, you have usually lost
your right to walk away unless there is a provision in the contract
that allows you to do so. That's another good reason never to sign any
document until you read and understand it first.

**Key #3: Be willing to admit what you know, and especially
what you don't know.**

When dealing with contracts, the worst thing you can do is to
pretend you understand something when you don't. Sometimes it
can seem that contracts are written deliberately to confuse us. In the
case of dishonest businesspeople, this can be true. But most contracts are written to cover a lot of technicalities that may never occur
but need to be addressed just in case. Your job is to make sure you
understand the basic points of the contract. Ask the other person to
explain the provisions of the contract to you. Get the outline of the
provisions in writing. Ask to take a copy of the contract home to

review. Don't allow yourself to be pressured into signing something right away to "lock in" the deal. I've seen far too many people who sign contracts thinking they're getting a great deal on a car or a home or furniture, only to find out they have agreed to horribly high interest rates or thousands of dollars in extra fees.

When reviewing the contract, make a list of any terms or provisions you don't understand, and ask for an explanation. Take notes, and let the other person see you writing things down. The written word is very powerful, and any notes you take will help if there is any disagreement. If you like, have someone else go with you when you review the contract. You might have a professional, like an attorney, review the agreement and explain the terms of the contract to you. The goal is not for your attorney to say, "Fine," and for you to sign just because you trust them. The goal is for you to understand what you are agreeing to. The more you know, the easier it will be for you to understand other contracts in the future.

What to Do If You've Been Ripped Off

What should you do when you've signed a contract or offer of credit, and discover you've been cheated? It can be very difficult to admit when you've been ripped off. Because of embarrassment or shame, many people keep quiet and never try to do anything about even the most unfair contracts. However, the worst thing you can do is to let embarrassment keep you quiet. If you believe you have been cheated or treated unfairly, take action. There are local, state, and federal organizations that oversee almost every kind of business and profession in this country, and they all have formal complaint programs. If the issue is important enough, you may wish to consult an attorney to see if you have any legal action you can take, either through small claims or other civil courts. But don't let yourself be ripped off without a fight. It may be difficult and unpleasant, but know that by going after these bad apples you may help not just yourself, but you also may stop other people from being victimized. Always know your rights, get them in writing, and then hold yourself and the other parties to a contract that is fair to you both.

Learning about contracts and credit is like studying the manual for the driver's license test. You may never need everything in the manual, but you darn well better know it just in case! And many of the lessons—which side to drive on, what red and green lights mean, how long it takes your car to stop—will become second nature as you get better and better at driving. As you learn about credit and contracts, when you get your first credit card or car loan or mortgage, you're learning "rules of the road" you will use again and again. Learn them well, and your time on My Street will be much more pleasant and secure.

The Heart of the Matter

➤ Learning to use credit responsibly is one of the fundamentals of financial confidence.

➤ You need to understand the importance of your credit report and credit score, and the creditworthiness of the lender.

➤ The do's and don'ts of credit are:

- Establish credit and use it responsibly.

- Look at the total amount of debt, not the monthly payment.

- Pay your bills on time, every time.

- Protect your creditworthiness.

- Know your credit score, and if it's low, do what's necessary to raise it.

- Don't mistake a credit limit for the amount of money you can spend.

- Don't get caught in the minimum monthly payment trap.

- Don't borrow more than your current earnings will allow you to repay in a reasonable amount of time.

➤ You also need to learn to understand contracts. There are three keys to keep in mind: (1) If you don't understand it, don't sign it. (2) It's your money/time/ decision. (3) Be willing to admit what you know, and what you don't know.

➤ If you feel you've been ripped off or cheated, don't let embarrassment keep you from seeking help. Know your rights, get them in writing, and hold yourself and the other parties to a contract that is fair to everyone concerned.

10

Basics #2: Investing in a Better Tomorrow, Starting Today

One of the biggest lessons for all of us from the past decade is the importance of planning and investing for tomorrow. Even though anyone who bought a home at an inflated price in 2006, or who lost 50 percent of the value of their retirement funds in the stock market corrections of 2000 or 2008, will tell you that no investment is guaranteed to go up or even to keep its value, investing is still your best hope of building a nest egg for retirement. But you need to understand how to invest, the kinds of investments, and the risk you're willing to take before you put your money into anything. Many people invested money without understanding any of these elements, and suffered greater losses than they might have otherwise. Now, I'm not saying that knowledge can prevent you from any losses. If you've heard the saying, "A rising tide floats all boats," you know that when the stock market plunges or housing values drop across the country, your investments will probably take a hit, too. But when you apply the principles in this chapter, you'll be more likely to lose less and keep more of your money even when the economy isn't doing well.

When it comes to saving for the future, there are three elements that are fundamentally under your control no matter what the state of the economy. First is the amount of *time* you put money aside for your future. If you start investing at age 25, you can endure more financial setbacks and still come out ahead than if you start at age 50. The earlier you start investing, the more you can save, and the more you can benefit from the power of compounding. Second is the *amount of money* you can invest each week/month/year. I'm sure you've heard the stories about average people—truck drivers, librarians, city employees—some of who never made more than $35,000 per year in salary. Yet because these individuals lived modestly, saved as much as they could, and invested wisely, they were able to leave millions of dollars to their families or to charity when they passed away. Even when your salary is low and your expenses are high, you need to make a commitment to investing in your future every month, no matter what. *You must actively participate in funding your financial future every day, month, and year.* You must establish the habit of saving and investing, so that when the time comes for you to retire or pay for your children's education, you will have enough put away to take care of those needs. Even more important, you also will have established the habit of living *below* your means—a good habit in any economy.

The third area where you have control is your *choice of investments*—the different financial vehicles in which you invest your money. What you choose should be based upon your investment goals, the amount of risk you are willing to assume, a good, solid understanding of the different kinds of investments, and the principle of diversification— how not putting all your eggs in one basket is the secret to greater financial security in any environment. The good news is that there are ways to save and invest that will protect you from some of the impact of financial downturns and help you take advantage of the good times.

Three Categories of Investments

Understanding investing and saving doesn't have to be difficult. Basically, there are only three types of core investments: *cash, fixed,* and *equity.*

#1—Cash

Everyone should have a certain amount of cash accessible for emergencies and general expenses. However, that doesn't mean you have to stash it under the mattress. Cash investments can be actual cash, savings accounts, money market accounts, short-term (less than a year) certificates of deposit or CDs, money market funds, and U.S. treasuries.

While cash investments earn you very little in the way of interest, they still should be part of your assets for two reasons. First, they have high *liquidity*, meaning you can access the money at a moment's notice—important protection against unexpected emergencies like job loss or illness. Second, they carry *minimal* risk that you will lose money on the investment. Low risk equals low rates of return; but in this case, the safety of the investment is what's most important.

Remember to keep your cash investments in insured accounts only. These insured accounts can be held at banks, savings and loans, credit unions, or in money markets at brokerages like Fidelity, Charles Schwab, and so on. Accounts at banks and savings and loans are insured by the Federal Deposit Insurance Corporation (FDIC); at credit unions by the National Credit Union Share Insurance Fund (NCUSIF); and at brokerages by the Securities Investor Protection Corporation (SIPC). Even if the bank, credit union, brokerage or other institution fails, your money—up to $250,000—is insured against loss.

#2—Fixed Investments

With fixed investments, you loan an organization or an individual your money, and they return it after a specified time period. In the meantime you receive interest at a higher rate than you would receive with cash instruments, because you lock in your money for a longer time.

Fixed investments include bonds (government, municipal, and corporate), bond mutual funds, second trust deeds, and any other long-term loan. With fixed investments, you get a better rate of return than cash investments, but you lose some liquidity—you can't get your money as quickly as you can with cash investments.

There are two important terms to understand with fixed investments: *principal* and *interest*. Here's how fixed investments work. Say you buy a 30-year bond from Company ABC for $10,000 (the principal), with a 5 percent interest rate. That means you are loaning Company ABC $10,000 for a term of 30 years. In return, Company ABC guarantees that it will pay you 5 percent interest on your $10,000 (or $500) every year for 30 years. Over those 30 years the company will have paid you $15,000 in interest ($500 x 30 = $15,000). *And* at the end of 30 years you will get your original $10,000 investment back when you cash in the bond. Not bad—for a $10,000 investment you will end up receiving $25,000 over the course of 30 years.

But what happens if you need the $10,000 *before* the 30 years are up—for your daughter's wedding, or an emergency, or a down payment on a house? You'd need to sell the bond. However, the amount you can sell that bond for will depend not only on the face value of the bond ($10,000) but also on current interest rates. Remember, interest rates fluctuate all the time. Say that someone has $10,000 in cash and is currently earning 3 percent interest but would like to earn more and doesn't mind tying up their money in a fixed investment. Considering that your bond pays a guaranteed 5 percent interest, doesn't it make sense that you should get *more* than the face value of the bond when you sell it? However, suppose that Company XYZ needs money badly and they decide to issue bonds that pay 7 percent interest (to entice more investors). If someone could buy a bond from Company XYZ that pays 7 percent interest, doesn't it make sense that you might have to sell your bond for less than $10,000, because your interest rate is 5 percent rather than 7 percent?

Here's the lesson: *the sale price of any bond will fluctuate with the current interest rates being offered.* With bonds or any type of fixed investments, when interest rates go up, the face value of the bond goes down, and vice versa. Therefore, if you sell the bond, you may have to sell it for less than you would receive if you held it until it matured. However, the value of a fixed investment usually doesn't change as long as you hold it until maturity, and fixed investments usually provide a better return than cash investment vehicles. Therefore, fixed investments are an essential part of your investment portfolio. They are great for income but not for investing where you want to see growth in your capital. For that, you should consider owning *equities.*

One last thing about fixed investments: you always need to check the creditworthiness of the person, business, or institution to whom you are lending your money. Too many people have lost money in so-called "junk" bonds or investing in a company that went out of business. Do your research on any company, business, municipality, or government institution before you invest.

#3—Equity Investments

When you make an equity investment, instead of loaning, you are *owning.* You buy something, like a stock, or real estate, or gold, for a certain price because you believe that it will become more valuable over time. However, the value of that investment goes up or down depending on the market. And, as the owner of that investment, you are taking all the risk.

The way most people can understand equity investments is to think of them like a house. When you buy a house, the amount you pay for it will depend on the current market. If you want to sell that house in five years, can you predict today how much that house will be worth then? Of course not. But here's the great thing about equity investments: greater risk potentially can mean greater rewards in the long term than you would receive with, say, a cash investment. For instance, imagine that in 1990 you put $10,000 into an S&P 500 index fund. That same year you put another $10,000 into a savings account that paid 2 percent interest. For the next 20 years you let your money sit in those two investments. By 2009, your savings account would still be paying 2 percent interest, year after year. However, even with all the highs and lows of the stock market over 20 years, your investment in the S&P 500 index fund would have grown an average of 8.2 percent per year.

Examples of equity investments are stocks, equity mutual funds, real estate, precious metals, and commodities. These types of investments don't earn a consistent rate of return (unlike a dividend), and the value of your principal (the money you put into the investment) can fluctuate up or down. You can sell many equity investments pretty much anytime you want, but it will be at whatever price the market wishes to pay. You may end up taking a loss simply because it's a bad time to sell that particular stock or mutual fund or piece of property. Because equity investments provide the potential for a better rate of return, you can do very well with them as part of your long-term portfolio. However, there is higher risk if you invest in equities with a short-term (that is, less than five years) perspective. If you think you will need the money within five years, you're better off keeping it in a CD, money market, savings, or other low-interest (but less risky) cash account.

Which of the Three Types of Investments is Right for You?

As much as investment companies or financial salespeople would like you to believe, there is no such thing as a perfect investment. All investments have some level of risk; all investments have advantages and disadvantages. But where you decide to invest your money should be based on the following three questions.

First, *what is the time horizon for your investment goals?* You need to know why you are investing, and how long before you will need the money, so you can figure out which investments will be best suited to your goals. For example, everyone should be saving and investing for retirement; but putting all your retirement funds in low-interest cash-based investments (savings accounts, CDs, etc.) would make no sense. For long-term retirement planning, you want to put your money where it can grow as much as possible until you need it. Suppose, however, your goal is to have an emergency fund so you could pay the family bills for a few months if you got hurt on the job. You wouldn't want to put that money into real estate because you might not be able to get the cash quickly enough.

The investments you choose need to fit what you want the money for, and when you will need it. If you just started working and want to save for retirement 30 years from now, for example, putting money into equities may be a great way to invest your retirement fund. But suppose you're saving for your daughter's wedding. She just turned 25 and has a serious boyfriend, so you probably will need the money sooner rather than later. A fixed investment like a bond probably wouldn't work. Neither would putting your money into stocks or a piece of real estate and hoping that the market will be high when you need to sell. In this case, the best investment might be in the highest-paying money market account, or a bank CD that pays a specific interest and matures (that is, you can cash it out without penalty) in a year or two. Above all, you want to make sure that your investments are *diversified*—meaning that you have some in cash, some in fixed investments, and some in equities.

The second question is, *how much do you know about this investment?* So many people say to me, "I don't own equities," and yet in their 401(k) retirement plan they have mutual funds that invest in stocks. When I tell them, "Your mutual funds are made up of different stocks," they look at me in complete surprise. I also see this lack of understanding with people who talk to me after consulting with financial salespeople. "My brother-in-law's guy told me to put my money into hedge funds," they'll say. "Now he says I've lost 80 percent of my investment. How can that happen?"

I'm not saying you have to be an expert in bonds or stocks, but you should know *something* about whatever it is you're investing in. This includes mutual funds that are offered as part of your retirement plan at work. A lot of people were burned in the 2008 downturn because they had invested portions of their retirement plans in several similar stock mutual funds without ever looking at the diversification in their retirement accounts. These people thought they were buying different kinds of stocks in different asset classes (a key principle of diversification, as we'll discuss later), but instead the funds all were heavily weighted with bank stocks or insurance stocks or auto stocks or other companies that took a real hit in the global financial meltdown. If they had taken the time to read the *prospectuses* for the funds—the mandatory descriptions of the composition, fees, conditions for investment, and so on—they might have understood exactly what they were investing in and chosen different funds. You must take responsibility for understanding anything you put your money into. If you don't understand an investment, either (a) take the time to learn enough about it so you're comfortable with putting your money there, (b) get professional advice on the investment, or (c) choose something else. There are lots of great investments that anyone can understand, but *you* have to take the responsibility for asking questions and getting the information you need.

However, beware of taking the advice of so-called investment "gurus" who offer free advice on the Internet, the talk shows, in books, on TV and radio. What experts tell you to do may not work in your particular situation. Also, most of the time all you're hearing is a "sound bite," a quick sentence or two that is easy for most of us to misinterpret. I know, because I speak on television all the time. The station gives me two minutes to explain what's going on in the market—but who can explain finances in two minutes? No one can. I try to encapsulate my own understanding in a very few words, but I say repeatedly that my comments are not designed to be financial advice. Yes, you can listen and learn basic principles from financial experts, as I hope you'll learn from me. But I wouldn't dare make specific recommendations for your investment dollars in this book. As I said in Step 4 of the Confidence Cycle, you should find a financial professional who is a Registered Investment Adviser, who will give you advice tailored to your specific goals, timeline, and knowledge. And make sure you understand their recommendations before you put a dime into anything.

The third question you should ask is, *how much risk are you willing to take?* Every investment carries with it some risk. Even if you put your money under the mattress, you could have a fire or a robbery and lose everything. Or if you put your money in a guaranteed bank account with a good interest rate, the bank could still go out of business and you'd have to wait a while before you got your money back from the FDIC. There are no completely safe havens. On the other hand, if you are willing to take on greater risk, you also have an opportunity to make greater returns on your money. The key is to determine your own *risk tolerance*—meaning, how much risk you feel you can comfortably take with your investment funds.

Your risk tolerance will be tied to five factors. First is the amount of time you have for your investments to grow. As I said earlier, if you're in your twenties just starting as an investor, you can take on greater risk simply because you have more time to make up for any potential losses. However, if you're in your fifties or sixties, you can't afford to lose much of your nest egg money, as you'll need it a lot sooner than your younger counterparts. Therefore, you will want to diversify your investments with less risk.

The second factor in your risk tolerance is your prior experience with investing. If you've been investing in the stock market for 20-plus years, you've seen your portfolio go through a lot of ups and downs. You may understand at this point that you can recoup a drop in the value of your investments over time. You also may have benefited from using losses on one investment to offset gains in another when it came to tax time. With experience comes perspective, and perspective may help you handle a greater amount of risk.

The third factor is your financial stability. If you have a steady job in a big, solvent company, you may be willing to take greater risks with your investments because you believe you can count on your income to continue. Or if, like some people, you have a spouse who also works, or you retired from one job and are collecting a pension, these additional sources of income may increase your risk tolerance. On the other hand, if your company isn't doing well or if you own your own small business and things have been tough, you may not want to take many risks with your investments.

The fourth factor is your emotional ability to deal with risk. When it comes to money, the two primary emotions that drive human beings are fear and greed. I see people who lost a lot of money in the stock market in 2008 and now they're so fearful that they won't invest in anything that doesn't have a guaranteed return, or at least guarantees that they won't lose their principal. Other people can sleep just fine knowing that part of their investments could go up or down 20 percent at any time. Instead, they may find themselves motivated by greed to chase the next "big thing" (like Internet stocks, gold, and so on) only to lose money because they bought when the price was too high. To be a successful investor, you must first learn to manage fear and greed. You also must know how much risk you can handle emotionally as well as financially.

The fifth factor is the amount of money you have to invest. Someone who has scrimped and saved for a year or more to put aside $5,000 to $10,000 is going to be more cautious and careful about where that money is invested than another person who already has $100,000 in a retirement account, possesses a $10,000 emergency fund, and now wants to invest his or her $5,000 tax refund. The more money you have already set aside, and the more you now have to invest, the more "wiggle room" you have to absorb some losses while seeking bigger gains.

Once you are clear on your timeline, prior investing experience, financial stability, emotional ability to handle risk, and the amount you have to invest, you're ready to work with a financial professional to design an investment strategy and plan that will help you achieve your short- and long-term financial goals. But any plan you create must follow one of the single most important principles of investing, one that will keep your money less volatile in almost any financial climate: *diversification*.

The Key to Financial Strength: Diversification

You've probably heard the saying, "Don't put all your eggs in one basket." Why? Because if something happens to the basket, you lose all your eggs. Diversification prevents you from losing all your "eggs"—the money you've worked so hard to earn. If you put your money into different kinds of investments (*not* different versions of the same thing), even if something goes wrong in one investment, the money you have in the other kinds should be okay.

Think of it this way. Suppose you invested all your money in a rental property and then the real estate bubble burst, or the tenants trashed it so it lost a lot of its value. If instead you had bought a less expensive property and invested the rest of your money in stocks, bonds, or savings, you'd still have some of your money left. Any one investment can go down to nothing, as we've seen with some stocks or even with properties; but if you're diversified, the probability is that your other investments will still have some value.

Diversification usually means putting some of your money into each of the three categories of investments, or *asset classes*—cash, fixed, and equities—that we discussed earlier. That way, no matter what the markets and banks are doing, your money is probably going to be okay (remembering, still, that every investment has some amount of risk). In truth, one of the basic principles of diversification is what financial experts call "negative correlation." That's a fancy way of saying that when stocks go up in value, bonds usually go down, and vice versa. If your investments are diversified and you've got money in all three categories of investments, no matter what's going on with the financial world you stand to minimize your losses at the very least, and hopefully to make some gains as well. And when the markets are going up, you can benefit from the "rising tide" that's floating all boats while you still minimize your overall investment risk.

The good news is that you don't have to build a diversified financial portfolio all by yourself. Many companies out there have different investment funds that are pre-diversified for you—they allocate a certain percentage of the fund to stocks, another percentage to bonds, and the rest is held in cash. You also can do the research yourself and put together your own "fund" by choosing stocks, bonds, and other investments. But most of us don't have the time or the inclination to put into studying the financial markets to the depth needed to make those kinds of financial decisions. However, a good fee-only Registered Investment Adviser can help you choose the investments that are best suited to your financial goals. But here's the bottom line: no one will care more for your money than you do. You need to take the responsibility of understanding exactly where your money is invested, how much it costs for this particular product, and how it fits into your financial goals.

Earlier in this book I reminded you of the old fable of the ant and the grasshopper—the ant continued to put food (money) away all summer long, knowing that the winter was coming, so that in the lean times the entire colony would be taken care of. But when it comes to your own investing style, you also should follow the example of the gray squirrel. Gray squirrels stash their nuts in many different locations—a few in one tree, a few in another, some buried in the ground, and so on. That way if a predator or another squirrel steals the stash of nuts, or if a storm comes and knocks down the tree, there is always another stash of nuts somewhere else for the squirrel and its family to live on. That's the key to successfully caring for your future: make sure to invest your money in many different vehicles. Keep track of each one, know how your investments are doing, and make intelligent choices if you need to move your money around. But never put all your nuts in one tree, your eggs in one basket, or your money in only one kind of investment. Be smart, and the "seeds" of your money will grow into mighty trees that will shade and protect you and your family on My Street for years to come.

The Heart of the Matter

➤ When it comes to saving for your future, there are three elements under your control no matter how the economy is doing: (1) the amount of time you have to put money aside, (2) the amount of money you can invest, and (3) your choice of investments.

➤ There are three main categories of investments: cash, fixed, and equity. Cash investments are very liquid but usually have a low rate of return. Fixed investments return specific amounts of interest and carry lower risk to your principal. Equity investments carry higher risk, and the value of your principal can fluctuate, but equities also may provide better returns in the long run.

➤ To select investments that are right for you, you must determine the amount of risk you're willing to take. Your risk tolerance is based on how long before you will need the money, your prior experience with investing, your financial stability, how well you deal with risk emotionally, and the amount of money you are investing.

➤ Diversification means putting your money into different asset classes, and choosing different investments within each asset class.

11

Building (or Rebuilding) Financial Confidence One Dollar at a Time

Life is inevitably a series of highs and lows, ups and downs, and each of us is fated to do well at certain points, and to face setbacks at other times. We all go through moments when our confidence is high and then in the next moment we must deal with challenges that shake our confidence to its very roots. But the key to long-term success and happiness on My Street is to recognize that confidence should have little to nothing to do with our external circumstances and everything to do with how we choose to deal with any circumstances that might arise.

That may feel like a tall order in the moments when you're facing the loss of a job, or a huge unexpected bill that you can't pay, or a home foreclosure, or your retirement account cut in half, or a divorce or the failure of a business, and so on. But remember once more the characteristics of the ant. It stores up food for the winter, and keeps building and reinforcing its anthill day after day. Then one afternoon someone (like you or me) walks down the street and inadvertently steps on the anthill. Catastrophe! The ant comes back from foraging to discover that everything it had built and accumulated has been flattened. Does the ant sit down on top of the flattened anthill and say, "I'm never going to recover from this"? Of course not. The ant starts rebuilding its home—because instinctively it knows that, first, it can recover from this loss; second, the only way to recover is to keep taking action; and third, simply by taking consistent action it will rebuild not only the anthill but its confidence as well.

Many people who have lost as much as the ant did when its home was destroyed simply give up. They lose their confidence and never make anything more than a halfhearted attempt to recover what they lost. But luckily, many *more* people have enough confidence, enough faith, to pick themselves up and to start rebuilding immediately. They understand that the only way to recover confidence is to keep taking action. They look upon setbacks as a chance to learn from their mistakes, or to learn how to protect themselves better, or to learn to take advantage of circumstances by anticipating trends as well as any possible challenges they might face. *You* must be one of those people. We all will face challenges that are guaranteed to shake our confidence. The question is, will challenging times break you, or make you? Will you use the principles you learned in the Confidence Cycle to remember what's really important to you (your life focus areas and values), set new goals that will help you get back on track, and then do whatever it takes to make those goals a reality?

Dealing with Obstacles to Your Financial Confidence

Life inevitably gives us obstacles, and they come in many different forms. As we've seen throughout this book, some obstacles are created by circumstances and others are created by our own beliefs and emotions. I'm going to give you a short description of different kinds of inner and outer obstacles that you may have encountered, or may be dealing with currently, so you can deal with them immediately. I can tell you from personal experience, it does no good to ignore obstacles, because they won't go away. Trying to make progress while ignoring your obstacles is like trying to run a marathon while ignoring the fact that your leg is broken. You're not going to make a lot of progress, you might cause permanent damage to yourself, and it's definitely going to be a lot more painful.

The best way to deal with obstacles is to prepare for them in advance. If you can anticipate the obstacles and avoid most of them, you will reach your destination in much better shape than someone who just took off on the journey with complete ignorance of all the potential pitfalls. As you read the list of obstacles, ask yourself, "Have I ever felt this way? Is this what has held me back? How has this particular obstacle affected me?" Then use these suggestions to help you deal with these obstacles if and when they arise.

Internal Obstacles

Fear: Fear can be a good thing when it causes us to look before we leap. However, for most of us it stops us from looking at all, much less leaping. Fear is like the tollgate on the road to financial confidence. We have to be willing to pay the toll, to (as a popular author once said) "feel the fear and do it anyway." Getting past our fears is the only way we'll get anywhere on the journey to financial confidence.

Limiting beliefs: Whenever I see people who just "can't" seem to make progress in certain areas of their lives, I always ask them, "What's the belief that's holding you back?" Inevitably there's something there. If you "can't" make progress financially, reread chapter 2 to see if you can identify a limiting belief, and then change it to a more powerful belief that will help you succeed.

Lack of clarity: If you don't know what you want, how are you ever going to get it? Fuzzy goals produce fuzzy results. Go back to Step 1 of the Confidence Cycle to make sure you are absolutely clear on what you want, why you want it, how you plan to achieve it, and how you will know when you've arrived.

Jealousy and envy: Negative emotions like jealousy and envy are some of the biggest obstacles we can face, and they are products of our tendency to compare ourselves with others. A better choice might be to look at successful people as trailblazers who have cleared the road for *you* to reach your goals more quickly. Learn from such people, and then do your best to exceed them!

Lack of self-esteem: When we first begin something new our confidence is often a little shaky; but a lack of self-esteem can keep us from taking the first step at all. If you are unsure of your worth or your abilities, remember that *your potential for success is the same as any other human being.* Believe in yourself, and believe that you are here for a reason. Make it your goal to be the best you can be and contribute the most you can give. When you do that, then you can be sure that you will succeed.

Lack of self-discipline: Self-discipline is usually produced by two things. First and most important is motivation: if you're motivated, you'll be disciplined. That's why the first three steps of the Confidence Cycle are designed to give you the kind of mental and emotional motivation that will make you want to make consistent efforts toward accomplishing your goals. The second factor that produces self-discipline is a system. Discipline is nothing more than doing what you need to do when you need to do it, and when you build the right systems, self-discipline will feel much easier.

Lack of commitment: This also is a matter either of motivation or internal conflict. Say you have a goal of doubling your income, but family is your first priority. If you think your goal will mean spending less time with your family, then your commitment may falter. One of the most valuable questions I teach people to ask is, "How can I (get my first goal) AND (get my second goal)?" Most of our goals are not mutually exclusive; it's just a matter of figuring out as many different ways as we can to get them.

Complacency: Too often we can become complacent when we've achieved a little success. We compare ourselves to those who aren't doing so well and feel pretty good. When that happens, we're dooming ourselves to a life of mediocrity. To achieve our goals and make the most of our time on earth, we have to fight our tendency to be complacent. We need to stay a little bit hungry in order to achieve our goals.

External Obstacles

Health-related issues: If you don't take care of your health, it can definitely prevent you from making progress toward your goals. But don't let ill health become an excuse for not taking some action. Do you know the story of Art Berg? At the age of 21, Art broke his neck in a car accident and became a quadriplegic. But he decided that being sick was not what he wanted his life to be about. Art worked hard to become a renowned wheelchair athlete, author, speaker, and teacher. He set a world record in 1993 as the first quadriplegic to complete the ultra-marathon between Salt Lake City and St. George, Utah—325 miles in seven grueling days. Art also married his childhood sweetheart and they had three beautiful children. The next time you think that there is anything that will keep you from achieving your goals, remember Art Berg, and keep moving in the direction of your dreams.

Unsupportive spouse or family: We all have people who feel connected to us, and sometimes those people seem to want to hold us back just when we want to leap forward. If your friends or family seem less than supportive, realize that they may be afraid of "losing" you on some level. The best thing you can do is to reassure them that they are still important in your life. Remember, step 4 in the Confidence Cycle is to Communicate and Collaborate—Get Buy-in and Build Your Team. As long as your friends and family feel you still love and care for them, and they recognize how important this new direction is to you, then usually they will be willing to let you pursue your goals.

Lack of time: This is the lament of the modern world—but somehow we always make time for the things that are important. If you have a strong enough reason and a lot of emotion attached to a particular goal, then I guarantee you'll make the time to make it happen. Even five minutes a day can make a major difference, and often five minutes a day can become ten, then 20, and before you know it, you will have achieved your goal.

Lack of money: I hear this from people all the time. They just don't see how they can squeeze any more out of their take-home pay to put into retirement savings, or to put toward their children's education. But even if you're struggling to make ends meet, could you put aside $1 a day without really noticing that it was gone? It all comes down to motivation and priorities. Keeping your goals right in front of you, and staying connected to how great it will feel when you see your son get his college diploma or when you enjoy a comfortable retirement, will help you postpone the small pleasures of the present for much larger pleasures in the future.

Lack of knowledge or education: To my mind, this obstacle is always temporary because we can always learn whatever we need to know to accomplish our goals. It's just a question of finding out (1) what we need to know, (2) how can we learn it, and then (3) putting in the effort necessary to do so. There are so many ways to acquire knowledge in today's world. You can read books (like this one); you can join a group of people who have the information you seek; you can find someone to teach or mentor you; you can get on the Internet and look up what you need to know. Pursue the knowledge you need as your first step in reaching your goal.

Lack of experience: Whenever we start something, by definition we're not going to have any experience at it. The "lack of experience" obstacle is really nothing but fear of failure in another disguise. Do me a favor: commit to being really lousy at something the first time you try it. The key to success is to keep trying. Eventually, you'll know exactly what to do and you *will* be great.

Keep in Mind What's Truly Important on My Street

There's an inspiring video that's been circulating on the Internet for several years. It shows a remarkable race run by an Englishman, Derek Redmond, in the 1992 Olympics. In 1985, at the age of 19, Derek had broken the English record for the 400-meter race. He set another record for the same distance in 1987. But he was prone to injury; he had to pull out of the 1988 Olympics, ten minutes before his race, due to an Achilles tendon tear. Five surgeries and four years of rehabilitation later, Derek was able to qualify for the 1992 Olympics, which was held in Barcelona, Spain. On the day of the 400-meter race, he was ready, and determined to win a medal. As the runners circled the track on the last lap of the semifinals, Derek was ahead of the pack. But 175 meters from the finish line, he crumpled to the ground, holding his leg. His right hamstring had popped. There was no way he would qualify for the final; his dream was over.

Most racers would have waited on the track until the doctors came to check them out and carry them off the field. But not Derek Redmond. He got back up on his feet and began limping, hobbling, hopping on one leg toward the finish line. He was going to finish his race no matter what. The crowd stared in disbelief and then began cheering wildly. In the next moment Derek's father, who had been with his son throughout his years of training and who was watching the race from the stands, pushed his way past the security guards and ran onto the track. He put his arm around his son and said, "We'll finish this together." Both of them were crying as they made their way slowly down the track. Derek leaned on his father as he took step after painful step. Right before the finish line, Derek's dad let go so his son could finish the race by himself. Then father and son hugged each other fiercely while the crowd gave them both a standing ovation.

Confidence needs to be built—or rebuilt after a setback—not by waiting for circumstances to be in your favor but by making the most of what you have and deciding to persevere despite the challenges you may face. And it's by facing our challenges, pushing past them, falling down and getting up time and again, that you build character—the kind of character that the crowd cheered when they saw Derek Redmond hobble across the finish line; the kind of character that we want our kids to emulate; the kind of character that turns you into a role model of success, happiness, and fulfillment for everyone else on My Street.

As I hope you can tell by now, this book isn't just about learning to create confidence and success in your finances. It's about building a life that is fulfilled on every level, in every life focus area that's important to you, in every value you want to experience regularly, and in every goal you achieve. "My Street" was never meant to be a place where people live simply because they are rich. I believe that people like you and me want to live on a street where we can take care of our families and enjoy our lives. My Street should be a place where people work hard and get paid for what they do, where families celebrate birthdays and anniversaries, where people share both their victories and their losses. My Street is somewhere that our kids can grow up in safety, getting a good education as well as a good grounding in the principles that will make them happy and moral adults. On My Street people are self-sufficient but neighbors look out for each other, helping anyone in trouble get over the rough spots so they can make it to better times again. On My Street people take the time to love each other and be grateful for what they have and what they can share. Ultimately, My Street is not a place; it's a community, one that I hope you will be inspired to join.

The Heart of the Matter

➤ Confidence should have little to do with our external circumstances and everything to do with how we choose to deal with them.

➤ The only way to recover our confidence is to learn from our mistakes, keep taking action, and try to anticipate challenges before they arise.

➤ There are two kinds of obstacles to building financial confidence. Internal obstacles include fear, limiting beliefs, lack of clarity, jealousy and envy, lack of self-esteem, lack of self-discipline, lack of commitment, and complacency. External obstacles include health-related issues, unsupportive spouse or family, lack of time, lack of money, lack of knowledge or education, and lack of experience. The best way to deal with any obstacle is to prepare for it in advance.

➤ When faced with challenges, remember Derek Redmond. Don't wait for circumstances to be in your favor. Instead, make the most of what you have and decide to persevere despite the challenges you face.

About the Author

"What do you get if you cross financial advice author Suze Orman, Dr. Phil, and Mexican revolutionary Emiliano Zapata? Louis Barajas."

—The Orange County Register

Louis Barajas offers financial planning with a human focus, one that serves average Americans who are struggling not only with their finances but with their lives. Louis Barajas is a man with a simple goal: to remove the financial obstacles to help working families and individuals live the lives they have imagined for themselves. Louis creates meaningful money conversations that draw out the root cause for the lack of financial security and deals with those issues head-on. His humanity-based financial advice works well for people making $25,000, $250,000, or millions.

Born in East Los Angeles, Louis is a living example of the American Dream of hard work, a successful business, and a rich family life. After some personal life-changing events and years of experience at major financial planning, accounting, and consulting firms in Southern California, Louis formed his own wealth planning firm in 1990. Since then he has created a special financial framework to help people who are inspired to create wealth and use their money to live a better life.

Louis is the author of several books, including *The Latino Journey to Financial Greatness, Small Business – Big Life,* and *Overworked Overwhelmed and Underpaid.* Over the past two decades Louis has become a nationally recognized expert in financial and small business issues. He was named one of the Top 100 Financial Advisers in the United States by *Mutual Funds Magazine,* and *Money Magazine* named Louis as one of America's Top Advisers. Louis served on the National Board of the Financial Planning Association for three years. He was named as The Small Business Journalist of the Year by the Los Angeles District Office of the Small Business Administration. He was also chosen by *People en Español* as a person making a difference in the lives of Americans.

Louis is a columnist and contributing writer for, and has been featured in, regional and national publications such as *USA Today, The Miami Herald, The Los Angeles Times, People en Español, Hispanic Business, and Senior Market Adviser*. He has provided his financial and business insights to national news programs such as CBS *Sunday Morning*, CNN's *Your Money*, CNBC, *Univision's Aqui Y Ahora*, ABC *World News*, and NPR's *Tell Me More*.

Louis graduated from UCLA, received his MBA from Claremont Graduate University, is a Certified Financial Planner™ and a Registered Investment Adviser. He and his wife Angie live in Irvine, California.

Become part of the My Street Money community!

Please go to www.louisbarajas.com to find inspiring stories from readers and register to frequently get updated tools and information to help you make the most of your money to live the life you have imagined for yourself.

To receive additional My Street Money bonus reports and to follow Louis, go to the Louis Barajas page on Facebook.

Check out these and other titles by Louis Barajas.

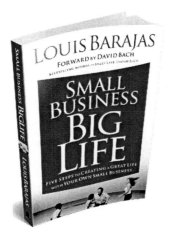
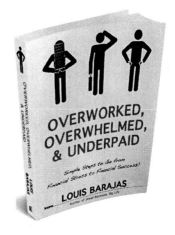

LaVergne, TN USA
29 March 2011
222130LV00006B/169/P